Bishop John J. Hughes,
His Church and the
Coming of Age of
New York's Catholic Irish

Bishop John J. Hughes, His Church and the Coming of Age of New York's Catholic Irish

Richard Daniel McCann

E-BookTime, LLC
Montgomery, Alabama

Bishop John J. Hughes, His Church and the
Coming of Age of New York's Catholic Irish

Library of Congress Control Number: 2012952816

ISBN: 978-1-60862-446-1

First Edition
Published November 2012
E-BookTime, LLC
6598 Pumpkin Road
Montgomery, AL 36108
www.e-booktime.com

Dedication

This book is dedicated to my own immigrant ancestors, who chanced the uncertainties of wild and foaming seas to seek out a better life...a life of opportunity, unfettered freedom, and the ability to fulfill one's fullest potential. Whoever I am and whatever I have become is owed to them. I thank you for your fearless courage in striking out into the unknown.

With All of My Love

Acknowledgements

This book would not have been possible without the able and cheerful assistance provided by the staff of the main New York Public Library's Reference and Reading Rooms located at 42nd Street and 5th Avenue in New York City. Particularly, I would like to thank the staff of the Manuscripts Division for their valued assistance in providing access to the personal correspondence and papers of James Gordon Bennett, Horace Greeley, and George Templeton Strong.

I would also like to express my sincerest thanks to Dr. Mark Bowles of the American Military University, who, from its inception, provided great encouragement with respect to this project.

Additionally, I would also like to thank Adjunct Professor of History at Kingsborough College, Dr. Herbert Gelbart, who over a period of many years, I had the distinct privilege of discussing, sharing, and learning a great deal about various topics in American History. His clear thoughts and insights have always been a source of inspiration for me. I always looked forward to and thoroughly enjoyed our exchanges. My perseverance in this project may be largely attributed to him.

Lastly, I would like to thank my wife Aine. She has always provided an environment that has given me uncompromising support for pursuit of my intellectual and recreational interests. She is truly the most unselfish person that I have ever known.

Contents

Foreword

Since the founding of the Republic, Americans have been a nation of immigrants. From the earliest days, German Redemptioners[1] crossed the ocean to a new land of opportunity and, after working off their passage, settled into a land where hard work, thrift, and honest living could achieve a measure of success. There were the Scots-Irish, a stalwart people originating from the province of Ulster in Northern Ireland, who in the early decades of the 18th century, adopted the tree-infested lands of Pennsylvania, later moving into the back country, the Carolinas, and Georgia. There were Dutch, Spanish, French, and Swedish settlers, all laying claim to the vast lands, not only along the eastern seaboard, but the southern and western parts of what was to become the United States. African slaves numbering four millions by the Civil War had been brought to America's shores in bondage, fated to be the human machinery that would support and sustain the cotton economy of the South. Considered chattel and being of a station in life not different from a farm animal or piece of furniture in antebellum America, they would eventually become a people whose contributions to American society would outstrip and begin to erase the degrading, inhumane, and criminal turpitude of their servility.

While the majority of Americans from colonial times through the 1840s were principally white, English, and Protestant, other immigrants coexisted peacefully and posed no great threat to the established order so long as they remained few in number and not heavily concentrated in particular areas to cause much care or concern among the natives.

But America's golden doors didn't always swing open to a warm and welcoming society. An often forgotten chapter of American history is the story of the pervasive and violent nativist backlash against the hordes of Irish Catholic immigrants, who fleeing the blight of the great potato famine that ravaged that nation from 1845 through 1851, sought refuge on the shores of America. This story, while much forgotten, is still playing out in American society. Deep within the American national experience is the old and potent mistrust of foreigners. The Catholic Irish, and later, Italians, Central European Jews, and in the present day, Mexicans and Central Americans, all to varying degrees, have been perceived as threats to the established order. Xenophobic fears of outsiders have long existed in our nation's history. From the dawn of the Republic, fear of foreign radicals, Roman Catholicism, and large numbers of foreign-born immigrants has lurked in the American psyche. The emergence of full-blown Native American movements in the 1830s and 1840s, as well as the Know-Nothing Party of the 1850s, had come in response to the nation's inundation with vast increases of immigrants, especially impoverished Catholic immigrants fleeing the ravages of famine in Ireland. With their campaigns and demands for restrictive naturalization and immigration laws, the intention of American nativist groups was to blunt the frightening impact of immigration through tougher immigration laws, restrictions on the process for becoming a citizen, and efforts to keep foreign-born persons out of political office. From the 1880s into the early years of the 20th century, nativist social reformers attempted to restrict the numbers of persons entering the United States on the basis of minimizing the impact of problems connected to crime, poverty, disease, and dangerous political philosophies, all linked to unrestricted immigration... or so went the rationalization for these measures.[2]

To the white, nativist Protestant, the Irish immigrants of the famine era were the most scurvy and contemptuous scum imaginable. They were destitute and Catholic, a religion believed by Protestants of the time to be anti-enlightenment, anti-progressive, and anti-Republican; its followers the cowed minions of a Roman dictator. They were drunkards and cast in ape-like depictions in newspapers and publications. Because of their Catholicism, they incited the fears long held in Protestant memory that had resulted from generations of bitter and bloody religious intrigues and warfare in Europe. The Irish were ignorant, unwashed, unsociable, lacking in the high Protestant moral standards of temperance, and totally incapable of being imbued with the flourishing ideals of democracy and American Republican virtue. They had to be stopped at all costs. In an age when sensitivity and political correctness were unknown, Catholics in general, and Irish Catholics in particular, were baited even by so-called respectable Protestants like the Reverend Lyman Beecher, who, reacting to the growing and aggressive evangelization of Roman Catholicism not only toward the lowest immigrant, but to Protestants as well, stated, "The Catholics have a perfect right to proselyte the nation to their faith if they are able to do it. But I, too, have the right of preventing it if I am able."[3]

The small community of Catholics in America had, for the most part, remained invisible in the first years of the new Republic, their numbers not representing a large enough threat to excite the worst elements of Protestant bigotry. The Catholic ecclesiastic leadership was, for the most part, quiescent, as it was a widely held belief that to suffer in silence for the sake of avoiding Protestant wrath was a far better position to adapt. By the 1840s, starting with the massive waves of utterly destitute Irish pouring through places like New York, the Catholic Church began a robust period of growth, and its growth was attributable not just to numbers, but to the new course of making itself a church with special outreach to the Irish, who represented America's first real body of urban poor. As African Americans would embrace their churches as a source of inspiration, protection, and succor during the Civil Rights movement in the South of the 1950s and early 1960s, the famine Irish of the mid-19th century would reconnect with the religion of their forefathers as a means of establishing community, identity, and, ultimately, Americanism in a new and hostile land.

John Joseph Hughes was not considered a particularly good church administrator. He could be obstinate and possessed a somewhat mercurial nature.[4] He apparently did not have a great concern for Catholics within his See other than for his own Irish people. Himself an Irish immigrant from County Tyrone, he had worked as a gardener in the seminary that would admit him as a student and from where he would take holy orders as a priest in the Roman Catholic Church. From early in his career, he was marked as a cleric of promise. He was not to be "quiescent." From the earliest days of his priestly vocation, he became a vocal and aggressive defender of his faith against the commonly accepted Catholic bashing of the times. His outspoken and eloquent defense of Catholicism and his own Irish Catholics was to eventually win him national recognition. With the sudden, massive influx of Irish fleeing starvation and death, the needed piece in the transformation of the Catholic Church in America from a minority, defensive institution to a growing and offensive institution was now in place. Hughes would take the battered human refuse of famine-ridden Ireland and build, within the time of his episcopacy in New York, a community of Irish who were not only more religious and devoted to the Church, but who would eventually emerge as patriotic and responsible Irish Americans.

Hughes was no glassy-eyed idealist. He explicitly understood that his people faced many obstacles in their journey to become assimilated into a strange, new, and hostile land. He knew that this could only be accomplished by being a part of, rather than apart from. He placed a premium on education; education grounded not in the Protestant world view of the America of his time, but rather, the values of Catholicism, which was the religious experience of the Irish flooding the American shores from the mid 1840s on. Catholicism had been the religious heritage of the Irish people since the time of Saint Patrick, and had been wrenched from them through centuries of oppression and a very conscious effort on the part of the English reformationist authorities to expunge the Irish of "Popery."

Hughes, while fighting the forces of prejudice and bigotry against his people, simultaneously, extolled the virtues of sobriety, good citizenship, and love of the adopted country. He ceaselessly worked to show that his people could, and would, be loyal and true

Americans. He condemned secret societies, which he saw as the residual debilitating effect of the effort of the English to suppress the Catholic faith in Ireland. He condemned the revolutionary sentiment that swept across Ireland and the continent of Europe in 1848, insisting that the true solution to Irish problems lay not with short-lived revolutions that were ultimately bound to fail. He was first and foremost an advocate of Americanism. He oversaw the painfully slow, but steady, integration of the first generation of famine Irish into the social, religious, and political life of the United States, with the culminating expression and proof of that devotion sealed on America's bloody Civil War battlefields with names like Antietam, Chancellorville, Fredericksburg, and Gettysburg.

The crowning recognition for Hughes, however, was not to be realized in his lifetime. The request to elevate him to a Cardinal was rebuffed by the Vatican, even after the request was formally made by the Lincoln Administration, as reward for his services rendered on behalf of preserving the Union. The accolade would be bestowed on Hughes's successor, John McCloskey, who would build on the work of Hughes and ultimately lead an Irish Catholic American community, who in the generation following the Civil War, would begin the period of dominance and reign of the Irish in New York politics, a reign that would effectively last for three quarters of a century.

To what factors might Hughes's failure to achieve the ultimate honor of becoming a prince of the Church have been attributed? He was, by all accounts, a popular bishop, held in the highest esteem by not only the Roman hierarchy, but the Pope himself. He was well-known and well-respected, as evidenced by the genuine affection accorded him by prelates of France, Spain, Ireland, and Italy in the course of carrying out missions to both raise funds for Catholic schools, and act as American plenipotentiary extraordinaire in European capitals during the Civil War. He was a friend of William Seward and was an intimate of Thurlow Weed, New York's most effective and influential political operative. He had been on good terms with Presidents Polk, Pierce, and Buchanan, the latter often making reference to how both men shared the same common Ulster background. In time, he would even achieve a grudging measure of respect from the men most prone to hate and vehemently disagree with him in the political arena; Horace Greeley, James Gordon Bennett, and George Templeton Strong, to name but a few of his most vocal antagonists.

No matter how the passage of time may have lent itself to possible explanations, there is one inescapable fact: the uncompromising leadership of John Joseph Hughes made possible the emergence of the Catholic Church in the United States as the largest and most powerful religious denomination in the country. He accomplished this task with the help of the Irish Catholic immigrant community, especially the vast numbers who sought refuge from the scourge of starvation of famine Ireland. In time, this group would not only be integrated into the system, but within a generation of their arrival in rags, dominate it.

Hughes was a prolific speaker and writer, and through study of his speeches, sermons, and lectures, one totally becomes immersed in the stream of passionate events and controversies that swirled around his priestly and Episcopal career. What I have attempted in these pages is to focus on some prominent events of Bishop Hughes's tenure, events that I felt were of significance in the formative development of the Irish Catholic community of New York, i.e., the school funding controversy, the establishment of a basic religious and social support network for an impoverished Irish immigrant community fleeing economic genocide in Ireland, and the contribution of Irish Catholics to the cause of the Union in the American Civil War. These were seminal events in the emergence of the Catholic Irish as loyal Americans, ready to take their place in the growing new land of promise they had adopted as their own. It is hoped this very modest effort may, in some small way, contribute to a continued and more in-depth discussion and appreciation of a truly great Irishman and truly great American.

This book has drawn heavily from the work of Father Henry A. Bran and Lawrence Kehoe, biographers whose own lives were closest in proximity to the Hughes epoch in New York. Father Bran was one of Hughes's priests and knew him in life. I am also greatly indebted to the work of Rena Mazyck Andrews, Charles R. Morris, Richard Shaw, Monsignor Thomas J. Shelley, William J. Stern, Dr. Patrick McNamara, and Robert McNamara, to name but a few of the numerous scholarly sources used in developing this story.

John Joseph Hughes's appearance on the religious and political scene of mid-19th century America was destined to prove apocryphal. His courage and tenacity in the face of the most virulent backlash against Catholicism and the Irish would forge an unbreakable link between the two. Through focusing on education, piety, and patriotism, Hughes would mold, out of rough hewn "Paddies," men and woman who valued faith and nation. While this story has been often repeated in the American experience, it is one still ongoing in today's Central American and

Mexican American migrant communities, both struggling to achieve equality and acceptance in American society. Regrettably, their experience can be likened to the same unwelcoming and fear-ridden spirit that greeted the Catholic Irish over 170 years ago, who too felt the lash of prejudice and rejection. The pages that follow are but a brief summary of that struggle, and of the courageous, yet very humanly flawed, son of the "Land of Eoghan,"[5] who brought his Church and his people to their rightful place at the table of the American dream.

Richard Daniel McCann, June 11th, 2012
The Feast of St. Barnabas

Chapter 1

"Do Not Forget The Charity That Is Due To Persons"

For Thomas Mooney, the mud-covered and stinking streets of Manhattan in the 1850s represented money to be made. As a cartman, that is, a man licensed to haul away the remnants of animal dung, refuse, and other less than appealing matter, Mooney was basking in the glorious experience of American entrepreneurship and socio-economic mobility. An exile from the great Irish potato blight of the preceding decade, Mooney represented the "new" Irish immigrant, who in barely less than a decade, had moved from a starving, unskilled, and highly vilified foreigner, to the first step on the ladder of a better income and life. In a well-known publication, Mooney advised his countrymen how the carting business was "the road to success...common to all."[1]

There were many more like Mooney, and in less than a generation's time, these same Irish, who had been considered by Protestant nativists the vanguard of the most contemptible lot imaginable, would assume a position of economic and political power in places such as New York, Boston, Chicago, and Philadelphia...a power whose durability would extend

1

beyond the cow and pig-filled lanes of 19th century urban America for decades to come.

While many of the Irish who made their way to America arrived impoverished, Englishmen, who earlier had stepped on the shores of Jamestown and Plymouth, were mistaken in the belief that "Paddy" was to be left behind in pursuit of a better life.

But not all of Ireland's arrivals in America comprised a ragged and economically deprived class of migrants. No small number of the earliest Irish immigrants coming to the colonies in the 1600s, numbering 50,000 to 100,000 persons, 75% of whom were Catholic, belonged to a more prosperous class. Many of these settled in the newly emerging mercantile hubs like Philadelphia, but most were Redemptioners[2] who eventually blended into the mainstream of society. Some of these early Irish Catholic immigrants became prominent citizens, like Charles Carroll, from whose family would come America's first Roman Catholic Archbishop and only Catholic signer of the Declaration of Independence.

Upwards of 300,000 Irish immigrants arrived in America in the 18th and early 19th century. These arrivals were of Anglican, Quaker, and Scots-Presbyterian stock. Many of the Anglicans and Quakers were from southern Ireland, but over three-fourths were Scots-Presbyterians from the province of Ulster in the North of Ireland. These stalwart Protestants were the descendants of the Tudor plantations who had come in search of land and religious freedom, settling first in New York and Pennsylvania, and later migrating into the wilderness back countries of Virginia, Georgia, and the Carolinas. Among their numbers were the families who produced no fewer than seven Presidents of the United States, Andrew

Jackson (1767-1845) among perhaps the most color-
ful and controversial of this esteemed group.[3]
In Ireland, significant changes in how landlords
utilized land commenced with the end of the Napol-
eonic Wars. The conversion from grain to cattle
prompted steep increases in the rents paid by the
peasant farmers, most of whom were Catholic. These
measures resulted in economic hardship and a
massive increase in the numbers of evictions,
triggering a substantial increase in Catholic immigration to America. In the period from 1821 to 1841, the
population of Ireland increased from 6.8 million to
almost 8.2 million.[4] The greatest increase of the Irish
population in this period was among persons who
owned no land and who were allowed access to a
landlord's holding only for harvesting his crops.
Partible inheritance,[5] early marriage, and high birth
rates increased immigration from 665,000 to almost
1.3 million in the period between 1831 and 1841.[6]
For those who remained in Ireland during this
critical period, conditions worsened. As land became
more scarce and the number of people dramatically
increased, the peasant population began to rely more
and more on the potato. Debuting in Irish agriculture
around 1590, the potato root grew with remarkable
ease in Irish soil. The potato fast became the principle
source of sustenance for the Irish people, with the
average Irish male consuming upwards of 14 pounds
per day. The planting of the potato was easily accomplished through the laying out of the seed potatoes on
spade-dug beds and then covered with earth. This
process came to be of increasing importance because
peasants had to devote most of their working time to
their landlords rather than the cultivation of their
own food. With the planting of the potato crop, even
the smallest plots of land could sustain large families.

Typically, a portion of the crop was used to feed livestock. Anything else produced by the farm, such as butter, bacon, poultry, or eggs, was sold for whatever money could be had. For the average Irishman, life expectancy at the time was about 38 years of age for men, which compared quite favorably with life expectancy on the European continent. In contrast to his English neighbor, an Irishman on average grew two inches taller.[7]

The role of the potato was prominent in the Irish population explosion; however, in 1845, the first of a series of catastrophic potato crop failures as the result of a fungus wreaked a devastating famine on Ireland. "An Gorta Mor," or the Great Hunger, as it was to be known down through the generations, was, for the Irish people, its Holocaust. The net result was a loss in Irish population between the years of 1845 and 1851 of two million people, who perished through starvation, fever, or immigration to the United States, accounting for almost half of all immigration to American shores during the decade of the 40s, and over one third during the 1850s.[8]

The story of this first massive number of desperately poor, Catholic Irish immigrants has long been shrouded in ignorance and misunderstood as the result of decades of sentimental rubbish perpetrated through depictions of reddish, round-faced Irishmen wearing shamrocks, green hats, and inviting the neighbors in "for the cup a tea," after searching for gold in the streets. At first, there was a sympathetic, and even proactive, response to the plight of the famine sufferers; with the passage of time, however, as the "human refuse" of Ireland began pouring through ports of entry such as New York City, the newcomers were reviled and scorned by their white,

Protestant predecessors, who viewed the invading army of Irish rabble as a legion of the Roman Pope.[9]

The hysterical, intensely xenophobic, reaction against the Catholic Irish already had established precedent in the United States. As early as 1834, nativist mobs had burned an Ursuline convent to the ground in Charlestown, Massachusetts. Throughout the nation, circulars stating "No Irish Need Apply," were posted in the doorways of shops and businesses, and nativist political parties grew in power and stature, claiming the membership of prominent citizens, even a former American President, Millard Fillmore, during the 1850s.[10] Up to this point in America's history, Native Americans had been openly hostile to Catholicism. Now, the displaced persons streaming to America provided yet another dimension in the arousal of nativist passions; that is, the newcomers were Irish. Poor, Irish, and Catholic were for a long time to be the ignition words for nativist, Protestant antipathy.

When the Irish potato crop turned black, the dynamics of Irish Catholic immigration were unalterably changed. Irish Catholics in America were not yet possessed of numbers that warranted undue concern on the part of nativist Protestants, but the potato famine was to radically change that. The Catholic Irish fleeing the famine were to become the most reviled and most unwelcome newcomers that America, up to this point in her history, had received. Possessing numbers that would represent a major challenge to the established order, the Catholic Irish were most vehemently deemed to be unacceptable and unwelcome.

Torn from their native land, strangers in a country that was both hostile and inhospitable, Irish famine immigrants soon began coping with the arduous task of assimilation into American society. The Catholic Church as an American religious institution was barely standing on its feet, when the cataclysmic events of mass starvation and flight of the Irish from their country commenced. Though nascent, the American Catholic Church was to provide the mortar that would eventually bond the broken bricks of identity for Irish Catholics, a key element in their eventual transformation into Irish Americans. Separated from their ancient religious traditions for over 150 years by way of harsh, anti-Catholic Penal Laws in Ireland, many of the new immigrants were barely Catholic other than in name only.

By the middle decades of the 19th century, the American Catholic Church was a long way from being the formidable institution it would become before the close of the century. In 1830, Catholics represented about 5% of the population, and by 1860, only 14%. There had only been two Catholics among the forty men who had ratified the Constitution in 1787, and no Catholic was to occupy the White House for the first 171 years of our nation's history.[11]

Far from enhancing the power and prestige of the Catholic Church, the destitute Irish immigrants initially did little more than to further incite the wild and hostile resistance of nativists. In response to this unparalleled immigration menace, nativists undertook to establish more formal organizations to "protect" American society from the onslaught of foreign, Papist influence. The Irish community in New York, however, was to be the beneficiary of a new kind of Catholic ecclesiastic leader in John Joseph Hughes. As an immigrant from Ireland, he was raised up from the same soil as the Irish immigrant community he was to so vocally and robustly lead in the new world. Describing Hughes as a complex individual would be a modest start. He was a self-educated, forward-thinking man, possessed of exceptionally good writing and oratorical skills. He was also mercurial, combative, obstinate, authoritarian, and unrelenting in the pursuit of his objectives. He was an autocratic ruler who had a rare ability to be, at times, hated by those who, by all accounts, should have loved him, and grudgingly respected, if not loved, by those prone to hate him. He was, in spite of his shortcomings, a man capable of establishing warm, intimate, and long-lasting friendships, as evidenced by his relationship with William Seward, as well as Seward's mentor and New York political strongman, Thurlow Weed. In all of his dealings, whether with dissident parish trustees, his own priests, anti-Catholic newspaper publishers, or the most despicable anti-Catholic bigots, he was direct and unflinchingly honest. His greatest attribute, however, was a fearless and, at times, defiant posture with respect to his Church in the face of anti-Catholic and anti-Irish calumny. He never backed down from confrontation, and in an era when men often expressed their feelings with bricks hurled through the windows of Catholic Churches and had torches ready to burn them to the ground, Hughes shielded his Irish immigrant flock with a tenacity that, even among the ranks of his most scornful antagonists, would earn for him grudging respect. If ever a church and a people needed such a person to lead, Hughes was ready to confidently assume that role.[12] In retrospect, it is easy to now see how the kind of leadership he provided was so critical and necessary not only for American Catholicism, but for hordes of hungry and fever-ridden souls who would eventually become a successful and respected community of Irish-Americans.

Hughes's brand of Catholicism was revolutionary to the American religious landscape, and by refusing to accept passivity and turning of the other cheek, he aggressively stood up to the nativist bigots of his age, forcefully challenging a hitherto acceptance in American society of both physical and verbal assault against Roman Catholicism. While other American Catholic bishops preached quietude, forbearance, and patience in the face of anti-Catholic riots that erupted and swept across the country in the middle decades of the 19th century, Hughes threatened to turn New York "into a second Moscow"[13] if his churches or people were attacked.

The force of his pastoral personality, the structure provided by the Catholic Church, and the people material provided by Ireland's starving masses would form the basis for establishing Roman Catholicism as the largest denomination on the American religious scene, a reality that was to have profound, long-lasting consequences on the social fabric of the United States. The American Catholic Church and its hierarchy was to be an "Irish" Church, and coupled with the maturation of Irish political acumen during the Hughes episcopacy, the Irish immigrants of the "Great Hunger" were to quickly learn the valuable lessons in the use and exercise of political power in their adopted land. As the Irish perfected the many nuances of this new found power, they would lord it over the heads of their once nativist oppressors for years to come, eventually achieving the penultimate symbol of their success...the election of an Irish Catholic to the Presidency of the United States.

To Hughes would fall the task of shaping within the hearts and minds of his countrymen the requisites for becoming good and loyal Americans. While this process of assimilation would be painfully slow and fraught with intense friction with native Americans, the Irish would eventually succeed in their adopted home, due in no small part to the single-minded effort of this aggressive and courageous Catholic religious leader. For Hughes, the task of articulating and giving shape to Irish Catholic issues in American society was equally important as the regrounding of largely unchurched immigrants into the Faith. From the time he assumed the reins of the New York Diocese on the eve of the great Irish famine immigration in 1842, until his death in 1864, Hughes would steer the New York Irish Catholic community through both the physical, as well as symbolic, attacks of nativists, doing so by developing a strong religious and social base through the establishment of Catholic schools, hospitals, banks, benevolent associations, and orphanages. These separate institutions would sustain the Irish American community not only in terms of their material needs, but foster a culture that would ultimately blend strong Catholicism with patriotism, love of America, and love of the Irish homeland.[14]

I

The crowd, estimated at close to one hundred thousand strong, mostly Irish, gathered in the fields of what would someday be known as East 50th and 51st Streets in New York City. The date of this momentous gathering was August 15th, 1858, the Feast of the Assumption. On this date, Hughes, now an Archbishop, was to lay the cornerstone of the new cathedral of the Roman Catholic Archdiocese of New York. For most of the spectators, the event marked a celebration of the triumph of not only the Catholic

Church, but of a much maligned race. Irish people had come to witness, with a burning pride, the physical representation of their Church emerging as a significant force in the life of New York City. What better way to demonstrate this power than by the raising up of a magnificent house of worship? In his Mass sermon on this most auspicious day, Hughes's high, clear voice resonated out over the massive crowd:

> "But when they say, you are Catholics, and we have to support so many of your poor, more than any other denomination, and would it not have been better to provide these, your humble brethren, the comforts of a charitable roof and home, than to waste so much money in founding what, no doubt, you intended as a gorgeous cathedral? When they tell you this, do not forget the charity that is due to persons; but, as far as the argument itself, laugh it to scorn."[15]

The spiritual descendants of St. Patrick had, by this time in New York City, traversed a hard fought path in reconnecting with their Catholic Faith. The newly arrived immigrants had undergone a gradual transformation involving the reincorporation of an organized Catholic Church into their daily lives, a Church that had all but vanished in Ireland in the preceding century and a half. Hughes would utilize the Church experience to not only reenergize Irish Catholics religiously, but to provide the stepping stone for entering politics and starting them down the road to becoming Americans.

The changes undergone by the Catholic Church in the period between 1815 and 1865 would be profound. At the beginning of the 19th century, the city of Baltimore was the center of Roman Catholicism in the United States. Catholics of the period were so few and innocuous that the French-born Roman Catholic Bishop, John Cheverus of Boston, as well as John Carroll, his Baltimore counterpart, were both viewed by the Protestant community as respectable gentlemen and assets to their respective communities. Just as its English counterpart, the early American Catholic Church and its hierarchy sought to avoid controversy with its more numerous and powerful Protestant neighbors.

Less visible than the more affluent Catholic gentlemen of the period were the invisible, yet omnipresent, poor immigrant Irish Catholics, who were just beginning to make their presence known in the cities of the eastern seaboard. Their numbers were to continue swelling until the great explosion brought on by famine in Ireland during the mid and late 1840s. By the time that the bugles of civil war ceased in 1865, the American Catholic Church would be the largest Christian denomination in the country, numbering more than three and one-half million members. Fueled by the influx of immigrants from Ireland, the new Catholic Church was to become a militant one, dominated by the Irish, who in the course of their assimilation into American society, were to challenge the "status quo." Irish Catholics, as they slowly began their rise in American society, facilitated the simultaneous rise of the Catholic Church. The Irish in America were to be a predominantly urban people, and the erection of large cathedrals in their cities would come to symbolize not only their undying devotion to the Church, but a symbol of their ever increasing influence and power in American urban life.[16] Given this volatile combination

11

of man and institution, the resulting anti-Catholic backlash was hardly unexpected.

The Catholic Church had been a bitterly persecuted institution in Ireland, and by extension, in the United States. What is critical in the understanding of how great the role the Church was to become for the Irish in the process of their "coming of age" can be understood in terms of Bishop Hughes's vigorous establishment of churches, and how they ultimately reflected a point of reference for the Irish immigrant community that was not only spiritual, but social and political as well.

To rechurch his community, Hughes needed to establish the church as "home." Whether built of wooden planks or bricks, the church building assumed primacy of place in the ramshackle living areas of the Irish. It was warm and hospitable, a place where one could come in from the bitter cold or pounding rain. It was a meeting place for neighbors, and it was there under the reassuring gaze of saints in stone or the saving visage of the crucified Christ, that the immigrants prayed in silence, sought solace, and prayed for deliverance from their inner most trepidations about life in a strange and unwelcoming land.[17]

Even though Irish Catholics had been forcibly separated from their native religious practices and beliefs through flagrant and callous British misrule, they did attempt to replicate some semblance of their religious experience from home in the new religious and church experience of their adopted country. They fostered their own special devotions. Piety was developed, and special emphasis was placed on receipt of the sacraments, especially Baptism and Confirmation. Attendance at Sunday Mass, receiving Holy Communion on a frequent basis, and going to Confession at least once a year were all a part of the encouraged discipline to be observed with respect to the nurturing of the Faith. The practice of the "Irish Wake," a custom brought from home, whereby the dead were laid out for days amidst uncontrollable drinking and ribaldry, was slowly replaced with a more respectful and reverential treatment of death, including the removal of the remains to the church, as well as the proper Catholic obsequies. Additionally, devotional practice, recitation of the rosary, establishment of religious confraternities, and the study of the Catechism became the corpus of a well-practiced religion.

As the immigrant community began to steady itself and grow in economic strength and confidence, they began to provide the money for the building of churches. Additionally, monies were sent home to help those left behind, as well as gather the latest information. The increasing mail traffic was the lifeline for a people separated not only by a huge body of water, but by a strange culture and its equally strange customs. It is difficult to imagine the tremendously confusing experience of the newly-arrived Irish in negotiating the bewildering conditions of life as it existed in the United States. As an example, the multiplicity of religious denominations and groups differed sharply from what the Irish had left behind. In Europe, religion, with the exception of a few dissenters, was a monolithic experience. In the United States, a variety of sects made up the population, with no preset social or economic lines of division. What made the matter most baffling was the fact that everyone in America associated themselves on a level of equality, a phenomenon that would have been totally alien in both thought and practical application, not only for the Irish peasant, but for the lower classes coming from any European country.[18]

Overcoming these complex experiences for the Irish would be accomplished by a combination of factors whose origins lay in the famine-ravaged land they had been forced to abandon. In understanding the rise of the Irish famine-era immigrants in places like New York, it is necessary to understand what preceded in their native Ireland. By the end of the 18th century, with the easing of many of the most debilitating of the Penal Laws, Irish Catholics entered into a dynamic struggle with their English oppressors for the granting of full religious and political liberty. In the Catholic Emancipation and Repeal of the Union with Great Britain movements, it was only natural that Irish Catholics would have turned to their Church and clergy. The most potent elixir for English disaster in Ireland was a disestablished Catholic Church, representative of the majority of the population in Ireland, with no standing whatsoever, coupled with the intensely nationalist aspirations of the very same people. Irish Catholicism and Irish Nationalism were to become united in a common cause. As Professor Jay Dolan wrote in *The Immigrant Church, New York's Irish and German Catholics, 1815-1865*:

> "An Irishman in America observed that the St. Patrick's Day Festival represents the two most prominent traits of the Irish people, fidelity to their faith and loyalty to their country... religion and patriotism so closely interwoven, so closely identified. The English, by banning both, made religion dearer and patriotism more noble. By placing the love of God and

love of country in the same category, it made
martyr and patriot synonymous terms."[19]

For American Protestants, the deeply imbedded
culture of God and country was one which created
instant antipathy and reaction against Catholics. The
exact opposite effect was to be experienced by the
Irish, whose exposure to the virulent anti-Irish and
anti-Catholic fervor of Protestant Americans served to
greatly galvanize them, a force well understood by
Bishop Hughes. As the Irish began the transition of
giving their love and allegiance to the United States, it
too was to be as fierce and uncompromising as the
love they felt for the Ireland they had been forced to
leave. Greatly understanding this potent force,
Hughes would harness these deep-running, emotional
feelings to build not only a powerful Church, but a
politically and socially-enduring Irish American
community and legacy.

II

In the decade following the Civil War, Fifth Avenue
was to become the premier avenue in the city of New
York. Its greatness and lavish wealth would be
marked by its magnificent buildings. The irony had
not been lost on anyone by the time of the dedication
of Saint Patrick's Cathedral on May 25th, 1879,
namely, that Hughes's cathedral sat like a jewel
among jewels, and that it represented a dagger in the
side of Protestant antagonists. Hughes's Church had
come of age.

St. Patrick's Cathedral was the penultimate
dream of Hughes, who would be dead fifteen years
before this great memorial to the Catholic Faith he

had spent a lifetime defending in both New York and throughout the country would finally be dedicated. In 1858, even Hughes's supporters thought the wastes of "upper" Fifth Avenue a strange place for the erection of a building that was to ultimately signify the arrival of Irish Catholicism in New York. As construction of the cathedral progressed at an agonizingly slow pace, it would become known as "Hughes's Folly," and readily received the revilement of the bigoted and openly hostile nativist press. The New York Protestant establishment opined the project a sinful waste of money; money that could have been more appropriately used for the care of and bettering the lives of the indigent Irish refugees still severely straining charitable resources of New York. Writing the day after the laying of the cornerstone on August 16th, 1858, *The New York Times* ridiculed Hughes's words as "but just one more example of bad taste, which of late years, has more or less characterized what his Grace has said or written outside the immediate sphere of his archiepiscopal duties."[20] It was a different atmosphere some 21 years later, as police began clearing the area around the cathedral for the dedication ceremonies. By nine o'clock, the Catholic elite had already commenced passage through the main doors of the imposing edifice.

> "The families disgorged by the carriages were expensively and fashionably dressed, the men in high silk hats and Prince Albert morning coats buttoned up to the chin, with a peek of stiff collar above and waistcoat beneath. Their wives were buried between layers of lace-trimmed jackets and vests, skirts blooming with live flowers, hats pouring out ostrich feathers; their young sons were in pleated

16

wool pants to the knee; their little girls buried
under organdy and chiffon. The men were
part of the elite...men with homes on Fifth
Avenue as well as Madison Avenue and
Washington Square. They summered on Long
Island Sound, Newport, and Nantucket."[21]

The New York Times, in a viciously sarcastic
attack regarding the day's celebration wrote:

"To native Americans, at least those not
Roman Catholics – and very few native
Americans are such – the dedication of St.
Patrick's Cathedral, with front seats adver-
tised at a premium, must have seemed like
some grand theological show, and the regular
sale of tickets completed the resemblance."[22]

From its beginnings, the Roman Catholic population of New York consisted of Spanish, French, and
African American members. From the early 1840s
onward, these names were being slowly displaced by
those of Irish origin. On the day of the cathedral
dedication, the descendants of these Irish were
participating in the dedication ceremonies. These
were the men with whom Hughes had cast his lot
when he arrived in New York. These were the men
Hughes enlisted for support in the fight to impose his
powerful will on the lay-controlled, dysfunctional, and
disjunct collection of debt-ridden parishes, hardly
worthy of the name "Diocese." These were the men
who would help Hughes carry out the massive
program of making the Catholic Church a theological
powerhouse in the religious, social, and political life of
New York, a Church that would help elevate his
people to respectability and prosperity.[23]

By the cathedral's dedication, this vast network of friends and benefactors, led by Hughes's successor, John McCloskey, who was to be named the first Cardinal Archbishop of the New York Archdiocese, as well as the first American named to the College of Cardinals, were at the height of their influence.

Even with the tentacles of nativism still stretched over New York, the leading Irish Catholics of the day were men who had acquired power and influence. While the major publications such as *The New York Times* and other dailies still reviled working-class Irishmen with the incorporation of cartoons and dialogues using exaggerated accents, the Irish of the late 1870s, for the most part, were far different from their famine-era predecessors.

The Irish had, by this time, started occupying positions that facilitated their climb in society, such as the teaching profession and police. Increasing Irish representation in the trades was also beginning to transform the complexion of the labor force in a growing metropolis. As Irish Catholic men of power grew more numerous, they were defined by certain characteristics, the most prominent being that they were, first and foremost, loyal members of the Democratic Party. Their hatred of American style nativism and nativists was equaled only by their unrepentant hatred for England. They were generous in support of their Church. They were ardent supporters of Irish Home Rule in Ireland, but were unsympathetic to movements that smacked of radicalism, secrecy, militancy, or rebellion.

They were universally conservative with respect to social issues, and believed that the key to success in America was to be found in religious faith, education, and discipline, not in social welfare.[24]

The attendees of that day were a study in the emerging class of moneyed and powerful Irish Catholic politicians, lawyers, and businessmen: Judge James T. Brady and the acknowledged head of the New York Bar, the elderly Charles O'Connor; prominent among the bankers were William O'Brien, John O'Brien, and Emigrant Bank President, Henry Hoguet; Emigration Commissioner, James Lynch, prominent Dry Goods Merchant, Thomas O'Donoghue, and the man perhaps closest to Hughes in the planning and ultimate bringing of the cathedral project to fruition, Eugene Kelly. Introduced to Hughes while still a fairly young man, Kelly became part of a core group of bankers and merchants Hughes was to utilize in the establishment of Emigrant Savings Society, out of which grew the Emigrant Savings Bank. By the time of his mature years, Kelly had become a successful banker and was a key financial advisor to both Hughes and his successor, John McCloskey. At the time of the dedication of St. Patrick's Cathedral, Kelly was seventy-one years old and sat on the board of the Equitable Life Assurance Company, Lloyd's, in addition to being a member of the Board of Education and a trustee of Metropolitan Museum of Art.

Along with O'Connor and Hoguet was "Honest John" Kelly. A trustee and patron of the cathedral, he had been handpicked by O'Connor and Samuel J. Tilden (former New York Governor and Democratic Presidential candidate in 1876) as successor to the scandal-ridden Tweed ring and first Irish leader of Tammany Hall. Kelly was a quiet and powerfully built man. He was representative of a politics that was to mark the Irish in New York and elsewhere in American urban areas as the true masters of the "machine." Kelly was to bring a political order to New

York that had never before existed, accomplishing all as the silent, string-pulling boss who was to dominate American urban politics for the next three-quarters of a century.[25]

Hundreds of priests in black cassocks and white-laced surplices proceeded down the main aisle. Bursts of magnificent color were to be seen by congregants as the varying red, purple, and scarlet vestments of monsignors, bishops, and archbishops passed in solemn procession to the main altar. These were the newly minted princes of a Church that barely a generation before had been under vicious attack. "With the exception of the German Bishop Heiss of Milwaukee, the Frenchman Duhamel of Ottawa, and Archbishop James Wood of Philadelphia, a converted Episcopalian priest, most of the rest were Irish: Conroy, Hanan, Healy, Kain, Kean, Loughlin, Lynch, McCloskey (of Louisville, Kentucky), McMahon, McNeirney, McQuaid, Moore, Mullen, O'Hara, O'Reilly, Purcell, Quinlan, Rogers, two Ryans, Shanahan, and Sweeeny."[26]

That all of this had transpired in a generation and a half from the arrival of Ireland's human debris was testament to the man whose vision, fortitude, and courage had supported Erin's huddled masses through the "starving time" was beyond the slightest doubt. The Irish had been beaten down time after time, but came back again; they had been rejected by their Native American neighbors, but yet were ready to answer the battle cry of freedom when men could no longer settle their sectional differences with words. They had fought for schools where their children could be educated with an eye toward sustaining and nurturing their Catholicity, rather than be subjected to the bigoted brand of religious values fostered and imposed by the Protestant elite. Where they had once carted the dirt and excrement of city streets, the Irish could now lay claim to rising in the ever growing and more diversified work place of New York. It was a day that marked the end of Irish Catholicism's cowering in the shadows for fear of incurring Protestant wrath, for now the great edifice of St. Patrick's soared ever upward in pursuit of the rising sun of opportunity, a new day and new era. Though anti-Irish and anti-Catholic bigotry still persisted in many quarters and would continue to rear its ugly head for many decades into the future, it had become less strident, and to some extent, grudgingly accepting. John Joseph Hughes, though long dead, was very much presiding over this triumphant day for his Irish American community from his place in Heaven.

Chapter 2

Holding On To What Little Remains

For the Catholic poor of Ireland, the cruel divorce of religion from daily life, reinforced by decades of English governmental prohibition, was to play itself out in America. When there is little left, a man will grasp onto whatever remains with greater determination. So it was with the Irish peasant, who divorced from the land of his birth because the alternative was starvation, held on tenaciously to whatever supports remained familiar, as he took his first steps in a strange and unaccepting land. Naturally, these thoughts had often turned to God, and with the heavy burdens of assimilating and adjusting immigrant ideas, customs and mores made religion more important and more necessary as a way of life. For the Irish immigrant of the famine era, once the last view of Ireland beyond the horizon finally disappeared, for most, never again to be seen, the reality of separation made many to cling more strongly to their religious beliefs to whatever degree they existed. For the Irish, religion and Faith was their only link to the past.[1]

John Joseph Hughes was born on the 24th of June in the year 1797 in Annaloghan, County Tyrone. In the formative experience of the man who would become the fourth bishop and first archbishop of New York, Hughes, as a Catholic, was to be made very much aware of his status as a second class citizen in the English-ruled Ireland of that time. At the age of 15, he experienced firsthand the cruel and unjust lash of the Penal Laws, when one of his sisters died and was refused the rites of the Catholic faith at her graveside because priests were barred from entering the cemetery.[2] The Catholic majority in the Ireland of Hughes's childhood had no rights which Protestants deemed necessary to respect. Controversies between Catholics and Protestants were fought with bitterness and ferocity in the area where young John Hughes lived, and bloody faction fights between Ribbonmen[3] and Orangemen[4], with their treachery and assassination, were frequent.

The best the priest could do was scoop up a handful of dirt, bless it, and then give to the impressionable youth so that he could sprinkle it over the grave. It was for Hughes a part of the bitter legacy that was to burn not only in his soul, but the souls of his Catholic countrymen, who for decades had languished under the relentless program of successive English rulers to extinguish forever the flame of Catholicism from Ireland.

I

The culmination of the Geraldine rebellions against Elizabethan rule in Ireland, coupled with the sailing of Phillip's Catholic Armada to bring the heretical English back into the fold, convinced Elizabeth that

an anti-Catholic buffer zone was needed to prevent
Spain from ever having the advantage of an ally in
Catholic Ireland, who always stood ready to pierce the
heart of Canterbury with a dagger.[5] Starting in the
early 17th century with the collapse of the old Gaelic
Catholic order and the flight of the Earls from Lough
Swilly, the unmitigated, relentless, and savage dis-
possession and expulsion of the native, Catholic Irish
began in earnest with the plantation of Ulster.
English settlers and lowland Scots were brought in to
take possession of the seized lands. While similar
plantations had been carried out on a more limited
basis in the Midlands and Connaught during the
middle decades of the 16th century, the Ulster plantation represented a more systematic and organized
incursion and conquest of Irish lands. Elizabeth, in
effect, had her buffer, and for the next century, the
systematic removal of and disenfranchisement of the
majority native Catholic population with Reformationist Protestants would commerce in earnest,
culminating with the passage of the infamous Penal
Laws against Catholics in the aftermath of the Treaty
of Limerick in 1691.[6]

With the defeat of the Catholic patriots who
fought in the gallant but forlorn effort to restore the
Stuarts to the English throne, the Protestant ascen-
dancy was complete. The enactment of the "popery
code"[7] and the anti-Catholic laws were instituted with
the aim of completely eradicating the Catholic religion
from Ireland. The Penal Laws forbade the practice of
Catholicism, Catholics from holding parliamentary
office, and Catholics from holding any government
position high or low, and it prohibited them from
entering the legal profession and holding a commis-
sion in the army or navy. Additionally, Irish Catholics
could not receive education, engage in trade or

commerce, live in a corporate town, or within five miles thereof, forbidden to own a horse of greater value than five pounds, purchase land, lease land, vote, keep arms, hold a life annuity, buy, lease, or inherit land from a Protestant, or rent land that was worth more than 30 shillings per year.[8]

Exclusion was further achieved by enforcement of qualifying oaths, which would prove anathema to any Catholic...oaths which contained such statements as:

> "I do solemnly and sincerely swear, in the presence of God, profess, testify, and declare, that I do believe that in the sacrament of the Lord's supper, there is not any transubstantiation of the elements of bread and wine into the body and blood of Christ, at or after the consecration thereof by any person whatsoever: and that the invocation, or adoration of the virgin Mary, or any other saint, and the sacrifice of the mass, as they are now used in the Church of Rome, are superstitious and idolatrous..."[9]

The English of the 17th and 18th centuries destroyed the Catholic Church. The faith remained, but the institutional Church was disemboweled. Catholics had almost no churches, no clergy, and hardly any organization to speak of. Mass was said in remote areas, mountains, hedges, and forlorn places by priests who were considered fugitives and subject to suffering death for disobedience in connection to conducting Catholic worship.[10]

It wasn't until 1794, with English Prime Minister William Pitt's establishment of a seminary in Maynooth, that the flow of Irishmen going to revolutionary France for training in the priesthood came to an end.

The Catholic Church in Ireland that grew from these beginnings, that is, after a century of calculated and blatant demolition by English governmental authorities, was one quite different from the historical Roman Catholic Church. It was a church in contrast to the Protestant Millennialist Churches of America, decidedly in opposition to the modern, liberal state. The basis of this difference had been the French Revolution, and the Irish hierarchy and many of its priests in the last quarter of the 18th century had been trained in France. It was a church that was separatist in its attitude toward non-Catholics. Irish Catholicism, in order to survive in a country dominated by an English Protestant culture, had developed many of the characteristics of English sectarianism: defensive, insular, parochial, and puritanical.[11]

By the 1790s, many of the Penal Laws in Ireland had been repealed, and Catholics were now able to engage in enterprises such as the establishment of schools, participate in professional life, and vote in elections. Preclusion from participating in the higher activities of life, such as sitting as elected members of parliament, holding a colonelcy in the army, or captaincy in the navy, were still very much prohibited. The remaining restrictions to Catholics were a bitter reminder of their still servile disposition in their own land, and were more grievously felt with the failure of Pitt, having promised to end these restrictions, in not making them come to fruition when the act of union between Britain and Ireland passed in 1800. Catholics believed that emancipation was to be complete; however, opposition from George III and Pitt's fellow ministers proved too strong, and the plan was dropped.[12]

II

If one name dominated the history of Catholic Ireland in the first half of the 19th century, it was Daniel O'Connell. Born in 1775, the son of a small landlord in Derynane, County Kerry, O'Connell would come to be regarded by the end of his illustrious career as the most prominent political leader of his country.[13] Called to the bar in 1798, he commenced his legal career as one of the first Catholics able to practice law with the lifting of the cruel prohibitions imposed by the Penal Laws. In the period between 1814 and his death in 1847, O'Connell was to successfully lead the fight that would effectively end legally sanctioned discrimination against the Roman Catholic population of Ireland with the passage in 1829 of Catholic Emancipation. Additionally, he would lead a movement geared toward the repeal of the Act of Union with England, thereby ending Irish subjugation to the Parliament of Westminster.

After almost a century and a half, the burning issue of the period in Ireland was the demand for the unfettered allowance of Irish Catholics to achieve full equality and integration into not only life in Ireland, but into the British Empire generally. While attempts had been made in the first decades of the 19th century to advance the cause of Catholic emancipation through the workings of a small and influential group of merchants, landlords, and professional men, effective strides could never be made on account of internal quarreling and failure to achieve a unanimity of voice with respect to Catholic interests. Successive British governments ultimately found an easy excuse for not taking the Catholic movement seriously.[14]

The dynamics of the Catholic Emancipation struggle greatly changed in 1823, with the establishment of the Catholic Association by O'Connell. Chastened by more than a decade of political action with respect to the Catholic issue, O'Connell had learned well from the experiences associated with trying to weld the disjunct and quarrelsome groups of well-meaning Catholics, who were ultimately sterile and ineffective in the effort to advance the cause. O'Connell sought to achieve success by introducing the concept of "mass organization." He began laying the foundation for building a powerful grass roots organization by institution of the Catholic rent. The subscription for belonging to the organization was established at the rate of one penny per month, an amount that even the poorest person could contribute. This aspect of broadening the base of the movement proved highly successful, because subscribers were buying into the organization, and, quite naturally, were far more interested in its agenda as a result.

The second master stroke utilized by O'Connell was to actively solicit support of the clergy. As the spiritual leaders of a repressed body of people, no persons in Ireland were more respected and trusted by the common people. The intensive confidence-building of the Emancipation movement, as well as its rapid growth, gave cause for Church of Ireland bishop, Dr. Jebb, to state: "There is what we of this generation have never before witnessed, a complete union of the Roman Catholic body...In truth, an Irish revolution has, in great measure, been effected."[15]

The Clare Election of 1828 was to provide the first real test for the electoral appeal and strength of the Catholic Association. Members of the British Parliament were obliged to stand for election in their districts if they held ministerial positions in the government. Vesey Fitzgerald, the incumbent M.P. and a landlord sympathetic to the Catholic Emancipation movement, had been named a minister in the government. He had been a sitting member of Parliament for over a decade, and was held in good regard by many of the tenants of his vast estates. The problem was that he had accepted a ministerial post in a government that was hostile to Catholic emancipation. The Catholic Association felt that it had no choice but to challenge the Fitzgerald reelection bid. There seemed to be no suitable candidate to challenge and beat Fitzgerald until it was proposed that Daniel O'Connell himself should stand in opposition. Through a quirk in the Penal Law, while O'Connell was prohibited as a Catholic from holding office, there was nothing that barred him for standing for the office. O'Connell announced his candidacy and headed straight to Clare. It was now that the organizational machinery of the Catholic Association would be put to the test. In marked replication of what Irish immigrants would repeat in a generation's time in American polling places, Association officials and parish priests escorted their people to the voting stations in disciplined, enthusiastic formation. The result had an inevitable effect...O'Connell defeated his opponent 2,057 votes to 982.[16]

The great victory of O'Connell and the Catholic Association posed a dilemma for the Duke of Wellington, who headed the British Government. While neither Wellington nor his Home Secretary, Sir Robert Peel, were supporters of Catholic Emancipation, both men were political pragmatists and possessed the kind of political flexibility needed in a situation to prevent a crisis. The intensive excitement caused by O'Connell's defeat of Fitzgerald created uncertainty as to just what the people might do, and the authorities, fearing the issue could possibly ignite into widespread disorder, were prepared to do the necessary to prevent chaos. Wellington was correct as well with respect to parliament itself, where a huge body of support existed for allowing Emancipation to go through. While O'Connell was viewed as a charismatic leader, there was no guarantee that he would able to control his people. Wellington needed no further persuasion in the wake of the Clare debacle. In the parliamentary session of 1829, a Catholic Emancipation bill was introduced by Wellington and Peel over a vocal minority, who protested and fought the measure till the end. No other course, however, now seemed possible, and with enough peers and M.P.'s to assure a safe enough majority in both houses, the Catholic Emancipation bill became law on April 13th. The main provisions of the bill consisted of the removal of all the remaining prohibitions against Catholics. While they were still barred from holding the Lord Lieutenancy of Ireland and from the Lord Chancellorships of both England and Ireland, they could be M.P.'s, judges, generals, admirals, and government cabinet members. The Catholic community gained in morale and dignity what had been stripped away from it since Tudor times. The Catholic Faith, native to the soil of Ireland since the time of St. Patrick, was no longer to suffer the shame and humility of being a second class religion in its own country.[17]

With O'Connell now regarded as the undisputed political master of Ireland, he set about to use his tremendous influence to usher in a number of critical and long overdue reforms. Through his ardent support of the English Liberal party, O'Connell was successful in the achievement of a number of benefits for the Catholic Irish, not least of which was the expansion of voting rights, the easing of tithes to the established Church of England, the cleaning up of the corruption-prone system endemic to local government in Ireland, and the fostering of greater impartiality of the constabulary in the enforcement of the law.

The euphoria of the preceding dozen years, however, was dashed in 1841 with the return to power of Robert Peel, an implacable foe of Catholic Emancipation. O'Connell, seeing the return of all his most ardent enemies, decided to embark upon what would be characterized as his greatest mobilizing movement; that is, the movement to repeal the union between Great Britain and Ireland.[18] To accomplish this, O'Connell created a Repeal Association, and, along with that organization, a subscription, or "rent," of the type that had been so successfully used during the Emancipation fight. Again appealing to the clergy, the natural leaders of the people, O'Connell fed into the newly felt and highly electric sense of national pride amongst the Catholic Irish. Lastly, the mass meeting was resurrected to draw people to a specific locality for the purpose of demonstrating both strength in numbers, as well as fostering unity. The key difference in the Repeal meetings was that they were much greater in size than the Emancipation meetings that had preceded. The Repeal meetings were also more numerous, with over forty-three taking place in the year of 1843 alone. By the staging of these mass expositions, sometimes numbering upwards of a hundred thousand persons, O'Connell believed that he would force the attention of the British government to recognize and act upon the will of the Irish people to recognize their status. Most importantly, O'Connell believed and practiced his form of political activism with peaceful means. He put the point clearly at the outset of the agitation:

> "The actual mode of carrying the repeal must be to augment the numbers of the Repeal Association, until it comprises four fifths of the inhabitants of Ireland...When such a combination is complete, their parliament will naturally yield to the wishes and prayer of an entire nation. It is not in the nature of things that it should be otherwise. Such a combination as I have spoken of was never yet resisted by any government, and never can. We are arrived at a stage of society, in which the peaceable combination of people can easily render its omnipotent."[19]

The largest of the monster meetings for repeal was to take place on October 8th, 1843. The meeting was to be held at Clontarf, selected to commemorate the defeat of the Vikings by Brian Boru in 1014. Just a few hours before the meeting was to take place, the government ordered the gathering to be banned. O'Connell complied with the government directive, always true to the belief that peaceful and non-violent means were the most effective. He ordered his people to not assemble.

In the aftermath, while the meetings continued and rent was still collected, the Repeal movement gradually began to fall into a state of internal disarray...In effect, the government had imposed its will over a powerful political movement without the shedding of blood. By the time of O'Connell's death in 1847, the Repeal movement had splintered into many factious dissensions and ultimately would prove a failure.[20]

In another sense, a generation of Catholic Irish, who had been participants in the Emancipation movement and the Repeal agitation, would be shortly boarding the immigrant ships destined for America. They had been the ready participants in the organizational efforts to achieve specific religious and political goals in Ireland. The experiences of Ireland would be of consequential value in the effort to organize and confront the nativist American backlash of their soon-to-be-adopted land. England had failed in "keeping the rogues in subjection."[21] Alerting his Chief Secretary to the threatening state of Ireland, the Lord Lieutenant, Lord Anglesey, professed himself little doubt as to the necessity of reintroducing into the country the Insurrectionist Act.[22] British misrule, as always, continued to provide the impetus for the Irish to carry the bitter and revengeful memory of their plight in Ireland, a plight that when replicated in America, would be answered with unprecedented defiance. The Catholic Irish immigrants from the famine era onwards, while poor in material measure, brought an ability for facilitating political and organizational action, which ultimately translated into the unified response to the hostile and depraved environment they found themselves in upon arrival in America. It was a response characterized by a deep commitment to helping their own. This commitment, coupled with the tenacious memory of their stolen Catholic Faith, was to be strengthened and augmented by a bold, new American Catholic religious offensive driven by Bishop Hughes.

Chapter 3

"This Is An English Colony, With Anglo-Saxon Contempt For Everything Irish"

The Catholic Irish of the famine were the most pitiful lot ever cast down upon the land. Many arrived in sickly conditions. It was a wonder that far more had not perished during the long and physically draining transatlantic voyage. The Irish lacked the education and basic skills needed to even hope to gain a foothold on the lowest step of a greatly growing and expanding American economy. Completion of the vast ocean trek left many in a deteriorated state, unfit for even the rudimentary agricultural work they may have been accustomed to doing in Ireland. Lacking skills and trades, large groups drifted into the fabric work of the expanding and equally desolate ghetto enclaves of their ports of entry. While some did manage to push on into the interior, the majority progressed no further than the dank and dismal "Irish" slums of the urban areas. Loneliness, despair, and wider alienation, fostered by disconnection from familial ties as well as submersion in an ever growing hostile society, resulted in excessive drinking and violence. Child mortality, the result of large numbers of children who made the crossing, was high...61% among those immigrants who arrived in the port of Boston.[1]

Atlantic shippers, though hard pressed, were quite resourceful in assembling a flotilla capable of moving the ongoing cargo of human beings, though under the most dangerous and unsanitary conditions imaginable. The lack of regulation facilitated a tremendous pressure on the vastly inadequate transatlantic passenger trade to put more and more vessels into service, creating travel conditions aboard old, dilapidated, and unseaworthy vessels that were inhuman. Many vessels rushed into service were transformed cargo ships, with no consideration whatsoever for people's needs. Steerage passage was fraught with a lack of clean water, lack of proper food, and lack of hygienic and sanitary facilities. Sickness, fever, and diarrhea were common. Cramped quarters below decks, especially for passengers traveling with infants or very young children, were stifling and oppressive. Women, in many cases, were literally forced to sleep while standing up, and by the end of the long voyage, people might be rising for the first time, having lay in their own excrement for weeks.[2]

For those who boarded the "coffin ships," the trauma accompanying the famine exodus was to leave an enduring legacy. Bitterness and resentment were fueled by the reality that they had been forced to leave because they had no longer possessed a means of subsistence in Ireland. Ultimately, it mattered little to the departed as to whether their fate was an act of God or part of some sordid evil of man.[3] For the Irish who survived the crossing, they were soon to realize that barely paved, dung-covered streets had replaced the gold. In mid-19th century New York City, the Irish

accounted for 87% of the unskilled labor force, and
their dismally low percentage of representation in the
larger industries such as the building trades and
clothing industry, was equaled only by their equally
dismal living conditions. The principle living area of
New York's poor Irish at this time was the infamous
Sixth Ward, encompassing the notorious Five Points,
which today would be the corners of Worth, Baxter,
and Park Streets, then Anthony, Orange, and Cross
Streets.

Here, the Irish generally dwelled in wooden tene-
ments, with children playing in streets that reeked of
a shit-smelling foulness that defied description, and
where cattle, dogs, and pigs roamed at will. There
were no indoor water closets or sewage disposal. In
the adjoining Fourth Ward, know as Sweeney's
Shambles, another 400 Irish families were as miserably housed as their Sixth Ward neighbors, while a
seven-story tenement on Park Street near City Hall
housed another 50 families amidst the worst filth,
garbage, and smells.[4]

Trapped in the worst conditions, toiling at its
dirtiest and most menial jobs, struggling to retain
some semblance of family life, many of the new Irish
arrivals slipped into alcoholism, insanity, or crime.

I

John Joseph, the son that Patrick Hughes and
Margaret McKenna bore, had been blessed with a
strong physical constitution, one nurtured and
strengthened by the diet of oatmeal, milk, potatoes,
wheat bread, and fresh butter that typified the feed of
the pre-famine peasants of Ireland. Though scarce,
the occasional poultry and fresh meat that young

John Hughes consumed on special feast days such as Christmas contributed to the growing of his body into the hardened stock of Irish farm folk who were counted among the strongest of Europe. As he grew bodily, he grew in strength and devotion to the concept of hard work, sport, personal improvement, and most importantly, love of the Catholic Faith handed down to him from his parents. Education was a local affair, received by John in the vicinity of Aligher under the auspices of Master Scott, and later on at Auchnacloy near the village of his birth. At a young age, he felt a calling to the priesthood, but the humble means of his family prevented a serious pursuit of studies. Though surrounded by a world of agriculture, John Hughes felt no inclination toward a life of husbandry. Not entirely certain as to what his life's work would be, he settled in with a family friend, believing that his true interest lay in the world and study of horticulture.[5]

Patrick Hughes, as a Roman Catholic, no matter how hard he worked his land, was destined to always feel the lash of punishment by way of his landlord's increasing of the rent, and an absentee landlord at that. The Penal Laws imposed a penalty on industry, ultimately increasing the level of taxation on the Catholic farmer's land, making "getting ahead" an impossibility. The Hughes family sought to leave a land where their Catholic Baptism rendered them inferior and lowly serfs, and where the poorest of Protestants could exercise a charge over the affairs of their Catholic co-religionists. Determined to separate themselves from bondage, though not all able to leave at once, Patrick departed in 1816, arriving and settling in Chambersburg, Pennsylvania.[6]

John followed his father to America in 1817. Upon his arrival in Baltimore, he gathered his bearings and proceeded to Chambersburg, where he found whatever employment he could to aid the remainder of his family at home. Finding himself tormented by the growing desire to answer a call to the priesthood, his deep longings brought him to the College of Mount St. Mary in Emmitsburg, Maryland. While initially turned down for the seminarian program of studies, he was hired as an employee of the seminary, ironically, to work as a groundskeeper and quasi-horticulturist. After a year, however, his persistence won him a place as a student. At the age of 26, when most men given to the priestly vocation had completed their formal studies and were actively engaged in ministry, young John Hughes commenced his priestly studies. Having been accepted into the seminary by John Dubois, the prelate that Hughes would both later serve and succeed as head of the New York Diocese, he commenced his studies with determination and diligence. As a seminarian, Hughes continued to build on his ability to be a writer of grammatically correct English. He achieved distinction amongst his peers in the seminary and was noted for his oratorical skills; skills which saw the emergence of oral argumentation with a mastery of diction and emotional power.[7]

Hughes was ordained to the priesthood on October 15th, 1826 in Philadelphia, and was not a churchman ever to be far from controversy. Early in his priestly career in the City of "Brotherly Love," the young Hughes quickly had his first experiences with the fluid anti-Catholicism of the age. His own battle against nativism can be marked from that time with his assignment to the rugged, mountainous area around Belford, Pennsylvania. Catholics in the vicinity were few, dominated in great numbers by the Lutheran and Calvinist settlers whose detestation for

Catholicism was rivaled in energy only by the tongue and pen of the young priest, who through his courageous, eloquent, and outspoken defense of his Faith, somewhat quelled, and eventually won the respect and admiration of his harshest antagonists, as well as the undying devotion and esteem of his own poor and small congregation.[8]

Though not aware of the implications with respect to his own future as a bishop, Hughes's recall to Philadelphia in 1827 was to be a time of great significance with respect to his witnessing a controversy that was to have immeasurable consequence in the Diocese of New York in a decade's time. Hughes would gain a wealth of experience relative to battles he was to fight as a bishop and archbishop of New York in the years to come. The dispute centered around the "Trustee System," a system that Hughes was ultimately to dismantle in order to create a strong and centralized Church in New York. Trusteeism grew out of the early practice in the American Catholic Church of allowing pew holders, or congregants who had purchased their own seating, to elect laymen to positions of control as far the ecclesiastic affairs of the parish were concerned. Trusteeism had its merits, as it was a means of providing lay involvement with the affairs of the parish, and, as trustees had invested financially in their church by having purchased pews, were people presumably with a greater vested interest in the continued well being of their church. One of the principle downsides of this arrangement, however, was that the system, in effect, denied control of many of the parish's affairs to the priest, or even bishop. As the Catholic parish system began to grow, especially in places like New York City, inevitable and serious conflict with this system began to emerge. Some parishes became highly factionalized, with one group of pew holders attempting to oust some trustees in favor of others. Parishes became highly factious, and in many cases, often turned into bitter political battle grounds. In some cases, unscrupulous and unprincipled persons took advantage of this situation and were able to gain leverage and control over Church property, priests' salaries, and even clerical appointments, this all in spite of the presence of a pastor appointed by the bishop.[9]

There was never a doubt in the mind of Hughes, already under consideration as a successor to the bishopric of the City of Cincinnati, as to where the true power within the diocese lay. In an ugly incident between the pastor of St. Mary's in Philadelphia and his board of lay trustees, the pastor became so frustrated in his inability to deal with his rebellious group that he left the parish to its own devices, a move which incurred the sharpest rebuke from Rome to the bishop and clerics incapable of dealing with such a matter. Father Hughes mockingly recalled in the aftermath of the incident "that the bishop should be bishop in spite of himself."[10] Giving greater vent to his own feelings on the matter, Hughes wrote to one of his former seminary theology instructors, Father Bruté:

> "What will become of the Church if laymen, sometimes as depraved as they are ignorant, have such influence in her government? What will become of the clergy, if they must descend from their sacred character, and become parties and tools of parties in the petty broils of contending rivals for the office of trustee? And for what advantage? Just to have the choosing of their masters. There is no remedy for all of this until the time shall

come to aim the blow, not at the branches,
but at the root of this abominable system of
trusteeing churches."[11]

For Hughes, the bitterness of this strife was to be
stored away in his mind until he himself was faced
with a similar dilemma in New York. The hard lessons
of Philadelphia were not to be lost, and when the time
came, as a step toward building a strong centralized
Catholic Church, Hughes was not going to be ruled by
the laity.

Catholicism was a religion under attack, and anti-
papist publications flourished in towns and cities
throughout the United States. In all the strident
editorials, Protestant defenders of traditional American culture warned of the resurgence on American
shores of the "Whore of Babylon."[12] The premier anti-
Catholic bigot, Samuel F.B. Morse, father of the
American telegraph, tapped out an anti-Catholic
polemic over the wires of his invention: *"Foreign Con-*
spiracy Against the Liberties of the United States..."[13]

In Boston, a mob of nativist rabble fuelled by
alcohol and incited from the pulpit by Lyman Beecher
marched to Charlestown and proceeded to burn a
convent school to the ground. The passions of these
marauders were further piqued by the mother
superior of the convent house, who warned that the
bishop could supply over twenty thousand Irishman
to the defense of Catholics in Boston. This threat
merely provoked the mob to more unbridled destruc-
tions.[14] What had prompted such incendiary reaction? These acts were directly attributable to the
ghastly and sensational details associated with the
false stories centered around the escape of Rebecca
Reed from an Ursuline convent. Miss Reed had been a
convert to the Catholic Faith, and in fact had spent

some months within a convent. The stories and experiences reported included life within a community of deprivation, which modeled itself after the Holy Fathers of the early Church who sought God by going into the solitude of the desert and mortifying their senses.

But perhaps the most destructive and lurid piece of anti-Catholic propaganda of the time in circulation was contained in a publication known as Maria Monk's *Awful Disclosures*. First published in 1836, nearly 600,000 copies would be sold by the end of the 19th Century. Maria claimed to have taken the habit, as would have been customary for a man or woman entering the novitiate period of the their religious training to do; however, on the night of her induction, to her great shock, she found that she, along with the other young nuns, were to be used in sexually servicing the voracious appetites of various priests and monks, who supposedly moved with ease through a tunnel that connected the convent with a nearby monastery. With such ongoing sexual activity, babies were born in the convent, with the older nuns in the community making a practice of baptizing and then smothering them, to insure their admittance into heaven. A nun, who protested this debauchery and horror was condemned to death by the bishop, at which point she was thrown down into a pit with a mattress followed by nuns jumping down on top of the mattress until she had been crushed to death.

The story proved to be a hoax, as the mother of Maria Monk confirmed that while she had been in a Catholic orphanage as a child, she has never been in a convent. She had never been a nun, but had become pregnant in Montreal. Brought to New York by William Hoyt, a profligate former priest of the Catholic Church, he introduced her to a number of gullible nativist Protestant ministers. Collectively, this group concocted the Maria Monk story and crafted the lurid depictions of sordid and immoral life in a Catholic convent. As to William Hoyt, he was believed to have been the father of Maria's illegitimate childhood, and when she left New York to take up with another lover in Philadelphia, the Protestant ministers who had conspired in the creation of the first round of scurrilous lies compounded the crime by asserting that Maria has been kidnapped.

In applying a standard of fair mindedness to the nativists of that time, one could look to the assessment of William Stone, New York publisher, no friend of Roman Catholicism, but one who felt greatly offended at the accusations being brandished in the hands of his own Protestant clergy and community. Seeking to conduct an independent investigation concerning the matter, he asked for, and received, permission to call at the convent where Maria Monk had allegedly suffered her ordeal. He persuaded the nuns to permit him to examine the premises, and in doing so, he discovered that not the slightest semblance between the actual location and the descriptions as provided in the book bore any relationship to reality. Stone, on the basis of his personal investigation, stated, "I most solemnly believe that the nuns and the priests are innocent in this matter."[15]

Suddenly, the various Protestant sects within the United States were coming to the realization that among them was a "living" Catholic Church, and this threat culminated in an ever widening and acceptable culture of violence against Catholicism with both word and weapon. Fr. Hughes became enmeshed in a controversial exchange of views with a man who fancied himself the plumed knight of American Protestantism, in 1830, committed to putting down the power of Rome. The Reverend John Breckenridge, a Presbyterian minister, challenged Hughes to discuss the question: "Is the Protestant religion the religion of Christ?" The controversy was carried on in the Catholic and Protestant newspapers for months, and consequently, captured much attention.

In 1834, Breckenridge again took up the battle and posed to Hughes another question: "Is the Roman Catholic religion, in any or all its principles and doctrines, inimical to civil or religious liberty?" Hughes, as the Catholic champion, once again stepped forward to respond to the Breckenridge proposition. The debate between the two men was published in book form in 1836 and widely circulated. But even though Hughes was early on demonstrating his oratorical and remonstrative skills in reply to the persecutors of his Church, this activity was not always viewed by the Catholic hierarchy in a positive light. One such person was Philadelphia's Bishop Kendrick. What precipitated the disapproval was Hughes's decision to make an address to the Philadelphia Union Literary Debating Institute. Kendrick made it known that he was thoroughly angered at continued oral debates, and he forbade the *Catholic Herald* to provide any coverage of these events for its readers. In directives that were undersigned by John Hughes, who was acting as his secretary, Kendrick took the usual route of the American Catholic hierarchy's response to bigotry, namely, to advise the Catholic faithful flock to simply live virtuous lives.[16]

The Catholic Church was ripe for men of ability to assume positions of leadership during its early stages of growth in the United States. It was clear Hughes had been marked as such a person, as evidenced by the fact that he was tapped not to fill the opening in Cincinnati, but rather, was appointed as Coadjutor of

New York. Father Hughes was consecrated Bishop of Basileopolis and Coadjutor of the New York Diocese on January 9th, 1838 by the man who accepted him as a seminarian, and the man who preceded him as Bishop of New York, John DuBois. The two assisting bishops at the Mass of Consecration for Hughes were Bishops Kendrick of Philadelphia and Fenwick of Boston in old St. Patrick's Cathedral on Mott Street on that frigid winter's day.[17]

The contrast between Hughes and the prelate he was to succeed was both startling and unprecedented. Dubois, as most of the Roman Catholic hierarchy of the time, had dealt with anti-Catholicism by admonishing the faithful to be forbearing in the face of persecution and to live more exemplary lives. Nativism aside, Dubois had encountered his share of difficulty within his own diocese in attempting to ameliorate the issues confronting the diverse Catholic population of New York, which included Germans, French, Spanish, and African-Americans. Add to this the burgeoning number of Irish, many of whom resented Dubois because of his French, aristocratic background.

Hughes, the Catholic leader, was to make a radical departure from this acquiescent and timid response. Between 1820 and 1830, the Catholic population of the United States swelled to over 600,000, and these newer Catholics were Irish. Hughes gained national recognition as a crusader against the rampant anti-Catholic bigotry of the age. Hughes rightly believed, with his experience, especially with the utterly destitute Irish of the famine, who would dominate the immigration issue from the mid 1840s until the Civil War, that the relentless barrage of anti-Catholic prejudice that was to greet the Irish in their new land was demoralizing and a force working to hold back their progress. To Hughes, it was the biting sting of English Protestant domination 3,000 miles from Ireland.[18]

II

The origin of American antipathy toward Catholicism and the Irish had its roots in two distinct traditions: one racial and one religious.

The Anglo-Saxon mythology of being part of a "superior race" had deep roots in the past of Great Britain. It was only natural that this same mythology would cross the Atlantic Ocean, where it was to give birth in America to a resurgence of the notion of the all conquering white, English Protestant overcoming the obstacles and cruel hardships of an unknown and untamed land. America was the inheritance of the Anglo-Saxon race, and although predicated on historical falsity, nonetheless gave identity to white, Protestant Americans in the process of forming their notion of greatness and sense of belonging to this glorious group. From the 17th and 18th centuries, the English, as opposition to royal absolutism became a firmly entrenched way of life, needed to show the roots and traditions of liberty. English parliamentarians attempted to explain the institutions of the country prior to the Norman conquest based on the descriptions of Germanic tribes as found in the writings of the Roman historian, Publius Cornelius Tacitus.[19] These same parliamentarians attempted to trace England's love of freedom to the Goths, a collection of Angles, Saxons, Jutes, and other primitive tribes that invaded the Roman Empire.[20]

This lofty notion of the Goths had gained little appeal until the appearance on the literary scene in

England of the great romantic writers of the early 19th century. Romantics formed out of the past a genus of Englishmen embodying what was to be the whole of their national character, an Anglo-Saxon people descended of the finest off-shoot of the Teutonic branch of Goths, and Englishmen believed their nationality was tied to this racial source.[21] That the original population of England from before the time of Julius Caesar's first invasion of Britain in 55 B.C. was Celtic was conveniently excluded at the expense of Anglo-Saxon myth. Caesar, writing in his *War Commentaries, De Bello Gallico*, and *De Bello Civili*, differentiated in great detail between the Celtic and Germanic tribes of Gaul (present day France) and the Druidic priesthood: "The Druids are a priestly cast. They regulate public and private sacrifices and decide religious questions. The people hold them in great respect. They decide all criminal cases, including murder and all disputes relating to boundaries and inheritance. The Druidical doctrine is supposed to have reached Gaul from its original home in Britain, and it is a fact that to this day, men going on for higher studies usually cross to Britain for this purpose."[22] In the later nativist condemnation of the Celtic (Irish) race as inferior to the Anglo Saxon, they obviously chose to omit that the Celts already had a long established deity, oral tradition, and advanced civil polity that had originated with the Celts of the late Iron Age, or La Tène culture, which for centuries before the advent of Christianity, dominated much of central and western Europe.[23]

The New Testament Book of Revelation spoke of the thousand year reign of the Kingdom of Christ, the defeat of satan, and the final judgment. This epoch was named the Millennium. Among the more prominent teachings of the Millennial tradition among

Protestants was that America, just as Israel, possessed a special place in the world as a "chosen
people." Americans were bound to fulfill their
destinies in a new land, perfecting the way before
them to receive Christ in all his glory on the day of his
triumphal return to the world. The Catholic Church
did not teach a Millennialist doctrine. Catholic
interpretation of the Book of Revelation was viewed in
allegorical, not literal terms, in Christ's defeat of the
powers of evil. The rejection of the Millennialist
doctrine was to impact the Catholic Church in many
ways, one being that it lacked the Millennial sense of
urgency possessed among evangelical Protestants to
remake the world fit for Christ's return. It also meant
that Catholics did not share in the special belief that
the United States had a special role to play, anal-
ogous to ancient Israel. While the various Protestant
churches had synthesized Christianity with the
Enlightenment's science, individual rights, and
progress, the 19th century Catholic Church of Rome
did not. In an age when the hopes of a better future
for Americans and their nation was entwined with
Millennialist hopes, Catholic doctrine accepted neither
the idea of secular progress nor the millennium.[24]

The Catholic Church was relying on and gaining
its growth through the countless numbers of immigrants seeking refuge in America, as well as its
evangelization of Protestants. Never before had the
native Protestant establishment experienced, with
such alarming rapidity, the spreading of the Papist
religion on their home ground. Never before had there
been a greater perceived threat to the fabric of
American democracy, and the fact that many of the
newcomers were Irish did little, if anything, to
assuage those fears. Catholicism and Irishness were
seen as one in the same. If America was ever to

achieve her mission in the world, Irish Catholicism would have to be stopped no matter the cost.[25]

III

The United States was growing exponentially. In New York City alone, the population was multiplying at about five times the national rate. Dubois had suffered a series of debilitating strokes, and his increasingly failing health forced Hughes to take over responsibility for running the diocese. He was named apostolic administrator in August of 1839. He formally became the fourth bishop of the New York Diocese on December 20th, 1842.[26] The New York Diocese in 1838 comprised all of New York State and about one-half the State of New Jersey. Within this huge and unwieldy territory, there were a total of 22 churches, many of which were in acute financial difficulty, with 10 having had been established since 1837. A total of 40 priests served a Catholic population of 220,000 out of a total regional population of 2,700,000. There was one religious community then in the diocese, the Emmitsburg Sisters of Charity, seven Catholic schools, all located in New York City, and four orphanage asylums, two of which were also in New York City. These made up the total of the Catholic charitable and educational institutions of the time; moreover, the churches in New York City were saddled by heavy debt.[27]

The first, and perhaps most consequential, challenge to Hughes's authority came early in his Episcopal tenure. In 1839, the cathedral trustees had a catechist who had been appointed by Bishop Dubois and ejected from Sunday school by the police. A pastoral letter, written by Hughes and signed by

Dubois, threatened the parishioners with an interdict unless they repudiated the trustees. With the memory of Philadelphia's contentious issues with trustees, Hughes took decisive action. At a church meeting, called for, presided over, and addressed by Hughes, the threat of interdict was driven home by the bishop. This was a pattern that Hughes was to employ more vigorously and aggressively as time passed. More and more, he sidestepped the trustee laws. He most effectively utilized the tactic when it came to dealing with financially strapped churches, predicating a diocesan bailout on his retention of control, leaving a lay board that essentially were figureheads, and nothing more. Henceforth, trustees would have limited oversight in connection to financial matters, and no say whatsoever with respect to clergy appointments. In the financially healthy churches, Hughes, by the sheer force of his personality, began to break the grip of Trusteeism in the diocese. That control of Catholic Church property was vested in the hands of one man, one bishop, was not lost on Protestants, whose alarm over such control provoked the kinds of controversy that would be the hallmark of Hughes's reign for almost a quarter of a century. Hughes demonstrated an unhesitating willingness to utilize the moral authority of his office to reassert the focal point of power in the diocese as belonging to the Church, and not the laity. In his battles with the Protestant establishment of New York, whether over funding for Catholic schools or defending his Irish Catholic flock against charges of disloyalty, or overseeing the political organization of his people to achieve a measure of social equality, Hughes's unapologetic invocation of his Church's power and authority was to provide the cement for building the blocks of a strong Irish American community in both the religious and civic realms. As the passage of time was soon to demonstrate, the days of Catholic Irish second class citizenship were to be no more.[28]

The early 19th century Catholic community of New York was one which resembled its English counterpart; that is, small, conservative, respectably middle class, and quiet. Into this group fit a number of earlier Irish Catholic immigrants. With the flood of new Irish immigrants and the radically proactive leadership of Hughes, the Catholic Church was transformed into an institution that served the poor and strove to make itself a visible and powerful representative body of that constituency.[29]

Hughes sought to make the Church more responsive to the material needs of the destitute Irish masses. He embarked on a vigorous program of increasing the number of parishes to make the Church more accessible to the Irish. Before 1844, there were a total of 14 Catholic churches serving New York, one of which consisted of French parishioners, and two of German. By 1844, all the rest exclusively served Irish men and women. Hughes himself was dissatisfied that this growth had not kept pace with the ever increasing numbers of immigrants, especially in the initial years following the failure of the potato crop in Ireland. Simultaneous with these developments was the realization that greater numbers of priests and religious leaders would be needed to minister to the needs of the growing numbers of Irish in New York. Paul Cardinal Cullen, Primate of Ireland, consummate Vatican insider, and wager of unrelenting war against the effects of English Protestantism on the native Catholic Irish in Ireland, had marked America as the fertile ground for the development of a new Catholicism, a uniquely "Irish" Catholicism, with its focus on conservatism, discipline, sexual purity, and special devotion to the Blessed Mother. Cullen and his fellow bishops had targeted America for Irish Catholic conquest. The robust transformation of the Catholic Church in Ireland under Cullen in the years between 1849 and 1878 was to not only have a profound effect on the Irish Church, but on the American Church as well, through the agency of countless numbers of Irish immigrant priests who were sent out to minister to their own community in exile.[30]

Irish Catholicism in Ireland was being transformed from a rag tag assortment of pagan rites and broken Catholic ritual, oftentimes lead by poorly trained priests, to a Church of magnificent buildings lead by disciplined and educated clergy. Mass attendance in Ireland, which had been extremely low owing to the scattering of churches widely throughout the hinterland requiring the rotation of private houses for Mass, gave rise to many abuses, including excessive drinking, fornication, excessive catering to the material whims of priests, and the lack of privacy in the hearing of confessions. Cullen's takeover of the depressed Catholic Church in Ireland was to have a profound impact not only in Ireland, but would be brought to a greater perfection in places like New York, and ultimately, to the greater American Catholic Church as well. For Hughes, the religious leader, no doubt greatly influenced by Cullen's sweeping reforms in the Irish Church, there was great clarity of mission with respect to the fractured Catholic Irish rabble disembarking from ships day after day in the port of New York. The phenomenon of almost 90% Mass attendance in both Ireland and America among the Irish Catholic population was a post Cullen accomplishment.[31] The suffering and horror of famine and the long memory of that suffering was to become the departure point for a more disciplined and purer Catholicism. To this end, Hughes was prepared to carry this idealistic mission to the extreme. There was no situation, no person, or no religion that was going to prevent Hughes from pushing the interests of his Irish people and Catholic Church squarely into the forefront of American life.

Hughes, as part of his commitment of giving higher education in the diocese a greater impetus, moved the diocesan seminary from Lafargerville to Fordham, which opened as St. John's College on the site of the Rose Hill estate in June of 1841, purchased for the sum of $30,000 dollars. The first president of this esteemed institution, later to become Fordham University, was the Reverend John McCloskey, the man who would succeed to the Archbishopric of New York upon Hughes's death in 1864, as well as being America's first member of the College of Cardinals. Hughes also invited the Sisters of Mercy from Ireland, and in doing so, created a new world of services for performances by Irish women. The shrill and often violent expressions of anti-Irish and anti-Catholic bigotry so common in the 1840s bolstered the latent devotion of the Irish to the Church. In New York, Catholicism was now assuming a more affirmative face. Hughes had recognized that the arriving Irish were largely unchurched, and he hoped to transform them into avid churchgoers. As a means of fostering the bonds between the Irish and their Church, Hughes would undertake the creation of an infra-structure of Catholic churches, parishes, institutions, and particularly parochial schools.

It was the contentious debate over the funding of Catholic schools with public money that was to mark the first real foray of the infant Catholic Church into the solidly New York Protestant power structure.

Hughes was determined to establish a position for his
Church and people, a position that would clearly start
them down the path to becoming full-fledged Americans. Hereafter, Protestant nativists were to understand that Irish Catholics were a political community
who were ready to start making their presence and
needs known.

The American Bible Society commenced a campaign in 1839 to insure the Bible was read in every
schoolroom in the United States.[32] In the largely
Protestant nation, there was no disagreement
amongst the various Protestant denominations as to
the soundness of this proposal. This sentiment was in
line with the belief that any education worthy of its
name was one with a Biblical foundation. In this
respect, Horace Mann, the father of the public school
system in the United States, had said that "Our
system earnestly inculcates all Christian morals. It
welcomes the religion of the Bible; and in receiving
the Bible, it allows it to do what is allowed by no other
system – to speak for itself."[33]

The one version of the Bible which was looked
upon by all of the denominational groups within
American Protestantism was the King James Version.
It was understood that by use of the King James
Version, there would be nothing in favor of or
prejudicial against any one particular Protestant
group, and therefore it was to be considered non-
sectarian in nature. With its universally accepted
underlying assumptions for all Protestants, it was to
become the Bible used in conjunction with public
education. The word sectarian, however, was soon to
take on a different interpretation; that is, as the
school funding issue started heating up, the meaning
of "sectarian" would come to be synonymous with
"Catholic."[34]

Consequently, within the common schools of New York City, and elsewhere, daily scripture readings from the King James Version of the Bible were required. Prayers, songs, and general religious instruction at odds with Catholic belief were the norm. Anti-Catholic sentiment extended throughout the school program with references to deceitful Catholics, vile popery, murderous inquisitions, Church corruption, conniving Jesuits, and the Pope as the Anti-Christ of the Book of Revelation. In the face of such scurrilous Protestant bigotry in the schools, Catholic parishes fought back by establishing their own Catholic-centered schools in response. By 1840, almost 5,000 children attended one of eight Catholic parish schools then in operation, while an estimated 12,000 more children of Catholic heritage attended no school or were forced by virtue of their having to attend common schools to have their faith depravedly mocked and insulted on a daily basis.[35]

The political contest began with the firing of the first salvo by the Whig Governor of New York, later Presidential candidate in the Election of 1860, and later Secretary of State of the United States, William H. Seward. Seward was sympathetic to the plight of immigrants with respect to their rights to receive the benefits of education unburdened by those who would seek to impose one rigid religious standard for all. As the newly elected Governor, one of the first things Seward did was to recommend legislation that would enable immigrants to be instructed by teachers speaking the same language as themselves and sharing the same religious faith:

"The children of foreigners, found in great numbers in our populous cities and towns, and in the vicinity of our public works, are

56

too often deprived of the advantages of our
system of public education, in consequence of
prejudices arising from differences of language or religion. It ought never to be forgotten that the public welfare is as deeply
concerned in their education as is that of our
own children. I do not hesitate, therefore, to
recommend the establishment of schools in
which they may be instructed by teachers
speaking the same language with themselves
and professing the same faith."[36]

With this opening, the Catholics of New York
forwarded a petition to the Board of Alderman of the
city of New York to receive a portion of the common
school funds:

"The Petition of the Catholics of New York
respectfully represents: That your petitioners
yield to no class in their performance of, and
disposition to perform all of the duties of
citizens they bear, and are willing to bear,
their portion of every common burden; and
feel themselves entitled to a participation in
every common benefit."[37]

The Public School Society provided the stock
reply; that is, any allowing of public funding for
Catholic education would eventually result in the
replacement of common schools, a notion that was
patently absurd as it was bigoted. The petition was
denied.

Hughes emasculated the public school philosophy,
condemning it as a system that corrupted Catholic
school children and assumed a confrontational
position. He sent a petition demanding that Catholics

be given a portion of state monies and was again denied. This time the reply came not only from the Public School Society, but from the Methodist Church, which utilized the opportunity to launch an all-out attack against the Catholic Church with respect to the murder of heretics and unqualified submission to the Roman Pope. The Protestant response lasted for days, with no discussion of any substantive nature concerning schools, rather than poisoning the atmosphere further with the typical charges of Catholic infamy and malfeasance.

Catholics were represented as irreligious and idol worshippers, bent on the murder of Protestants. They were castigated as drunkards and breeders of violence, a slur aimed primarily at the publicly perceived coarse and crude lower class Irish immigrant. The Irish, depicted as ape-like in illustrations, were incapable, so claimed the established nativist Protestants, of engaging in the institutions of democracy, and followed a religion that was perceived as anti-republican and under the command of a Roman dictator.

On July 20th, 1840, Hughes himself asked the question before a packed school house hall attached to St. Patrick's Church:

> "It is the sacred right of every man to educate his own children, and when these are the consequences that follow this system of common school education, is it just to tax a man for its support, while its tendency was to draw away the mind of his child from the religion which he professed and which he desired to teach him?"[38]

In this new arena, Hughes put at his disposal the effective oratorical gifts he had been cultivating for years. He was not above skillfully utilizing controversy to advance his causes, and his harshest critics through the years would claim his method and tactics were sheer demagoguery; however, there started to emerge inescapable realities, the likes of which could no longer be ignored by those individuals who considered Hughes and his Church the "enemy." Firstly, nativists were slowly becoming more circumspect in dealings with this combative Irishman. Though stridency in the attack on Catholicism was not abating, Hughes, as a secondary consequence of the school funds debate, was forcing his opponents to acknowledge that the Roman Catholic Church was slowly gaining in size and strength, and that the Church now had a leader prepared to aggressively fight for Catholic issues. In time, they would even grow to accord him a grudging respect. Governor Seward supported the Catholic position, even though the state legislature and the city alderman sharply disagreed with him. In April of 1841, Seward's Secretary of State, John C. Spencer, ex officio superintendent of public schools, drafted and submitted a report to the state senate on the issue. The paper supported the legitimacy of the right of Catholics to be recipients of public monies for their schools. Spencer went on to say, in effect, that the argument connected to the sectarian nature of Catholic education was specious, as all forms of instruction were in fact sectarian in one way or another. Spencer proposed that the New York City School System be turned over to a board of commissioners, who would be charged with matters pertaining to instruction. The issue of religious matters, including, of course, religious instruction, would be left to the individual trustees of the schools.

The legislature stalled with respect to Spencer's recommendations, attempting to put off any final decision for as long as possible. When neither Democratic nor Whig candidates for election endorsed any of Spencer's proposals, Hughes initiated a radical departure from what had been the Catholic Church's hiding in the wings approach to Catholic issues; namely, he boldly sponsored a slate of political candidates for the New York legislature. The slate, to be known as the Carrol Hall candidates, were entered just four days before the elections were to be held, and created horror within the Protestant community. Hughes was banking on the ballot box to make his point, and while some thought the move calamitous, it was a major step in the evolution of a Church and her people. In the finest Republican tradition, the Irish were learning the power of the "vote" in America. The Catholic editor of the *New York Herald*, James Gordon Bennett, a man whom Hughes would cross swords with on many issues even though they were coreligionists, excoriated Hughes for the political tactics utilized in trying to organize Irish Catholics to function as a district political party, which could be bartered to the Whigs or Locofocos[39] at the wave of his crozier.

Bennett observed in the Herald: "The whole thing from beginning to end is only a preposterous insult to the common sense of an intelligent community. To all minds of intelligence, it will, after the election is over, reduce Bishop Hughes to the lowest state of degradation and contempt. He has shown himself to be utterly deficient in honesty or in common sense. There is no alternative on which to hang his crozier. If he meant seriously, in a Protestant country, to

succeed in his project, he took the very method that
would forever put a barrier between his Church and
the claim on the School Fund. One of the first
principles of American freedom is to keep distinct the
institutions of Church and State. No element of
liberty is more deeply imbued in the American mind
than this is. How, then, in such a happy, and free,
and positive condition of public opinion, could Bishop
Hughes expect that if the Church of Rome had a favor
to ask of a Protestant country, the best method to
acquire it was to trample this holy principle under
foot, and organize his Church into a political club."[40]

In spite of the timing, the tactic worked, and the
"Carroll Hall" candidates polled enough votes to put
an end to further discussion of using public funds for
aiding any school, Catholic or otherwise. At the next
session of the legislature, the pro Protestant Public
School Society was, in effect, no longer the governing
body for common schools in New York City. An
entirely new Board of Education had been created
and voted in. The new law provided that no school
providing religious, sectarian doctrine of any kind
would receive any portion of school monies to be
administered under this act. New York State, in effect,
became the first of the original thirteen states in the
union to prohibit the teaching of religion of any kind
in the public schools.

The aftermath of this momentous decision was
the stoning and breaking of windows in the residence
of Bishop Hughes by mobs of nativist ruffians. The
Episcopalian activist, George Templeton Strong, a
nativist who would come to be a noted and respected
member of the New York Bar, noted in his diary of
April 13th, 1842: "We had some hard fighting
yesterday in the Bloody Sixth, and a no-popery riot
last night, including a vigorous attack on the Roman

Catholic Cathedral with bricks and bats and howls, and a hostile demonstration on Hughes's episcopal palace, terminating in broken windows and damaged furniture. Also, the Spartan Band got into the Sixth Ward Hotel, as the no-popery rioters of old did in 'the Maypole,' and 'made a noise and broke things' in great style. Well, this is the beginning of the end, the first fruits of that very abominable tree – the School Bill."[41]

Hughes's victory had been substantial and significant, and while Protestant trustees could, and would, no doubt remain influential with respect to school curriculum, "Catholic" education would never again be denied Catholic children for want of their own schools. The display of such awesome political power at a time when the numbers of Catholics in New York was only beginning to swell was unnerving to nativist population. It was an omen of things to come.

Hughes set about creating his own school system. The school aid controversy demonstrated that the Irish and their Church were to be from here out a force to be reckoned with. From the mid 1840s until the Civil War, the exploding number of Irish Catholics fleeing the famine would both greatly test, as well as solidify, that force. The New York setting and the massive numbers of arriving immigrants fleeing famine and disease in Ireland made the establishment of institutions needed to ease the difficulties of immigration easier for moving out of poverty. Hughes was instrumental in establishing and overseeing a combination of aid societies, cultural, and social organizations designed to create a sense of cohesion in a new and unwelcoming world. The parish became a focal point of this activity, and in creating a sense of identity with a Church and a parish, a highly successful network began to slowly emerge that would lift the immigrant Irish from their poverty. Sending his priests out among the community, the Irish were encouraged to engage in frequent sacramental confessions, Mass attendance, devotions, and abstinence from consumption of alcohol. The renewed Church experience long lost under English oppression in Ireland and coupled with the ever increasing number of cultural and social organizations, the new immigrants were ultimately redefining themselves. Between 1846 and 1851, over one million people would leave Ireland, and in places like New York, the numbers of Catholic Irish immigrants was soon to catch up and surpass those of Protestants. The numbers, the Church, and newly evolving social structure, while not alone responsible for lifting the Irish masses out of the grip of living on the fringe and lowest rung of American society, in fact served to solidly establish the Irish into the urban structure and ultimately define them as a "group." The Irish were slowly bridging the gap between being immigrants to being settled in their new land.

Still, the Protestant clergy regularly engaged in the castigation of the growing Catholic community as idolatrous, popery, or the "beast." Even respected and influential Protestant ministers as the Reverend Lyman Beecher participated in this baiting of Catholics. George Templeton Strong's personal diary entry of March 17th, 1838 summed up the contempt with which Catholicism and its clergy were viewed by the established nativist community of the time:

"With Chittenden up to St. Patrick's Cathedral, this being St. Patrick's Day, to hear and see the services in his honor; the cathedral was crowded, the aisles jammed, but we had a pew (locked) nearly to ourselves and got along right comfortably. Mass by Bishop Hughes and clergy...music tolerable...The sermon was immensely absurd-out powered Powers himself. I never heard a comparable farrago, nonsense, falsehood, blunder, Hibernicism, bombast, nonsense, fun, flummery, bad grammar, false logic and stuff. The preacher was a raw paddy apparently, named Byrnes."[42]

The 1840s and 50s were marked by a continuous tension and friction between nativist and immigrant. Coupled with economic rivalry stemming from competition for jobs, the two groups lived in a high degree of social separation...perhaps even segregation. The Democratic Party tradition since Thomas Jefferson's time has been more cosmopolitan in outlook, less sectarian, and more concerned about the welfare of common people. This reality insured that when the Irish began their entry into American political life, they would choose to become Democrats. Like it or not, the Whigs were guardians of the more aristocratic outlook, the 18th century Puritan tradition of New England, and also supported a church state establishment. The notion of the spiritually elect was the underpinning of their moral outlook. Consequently, both groups were locked into viewing one another with intense distrust and hostility. Many natives regarded Irish Catholics as intruders and treated them as inferiors.

The Irish, in turn, deeply resented the flagrant discrimination and persecution which they experienced at the hands of the Yankees. The Whigs formed what was perceived as the propertied class, and firmly held on to the preservation of Anglo-

Protestant tradition. This was most intuitively understood by the hordes of poor Catholic Irish, who in
looking at the Whig political establishment, saw
landlords and their hereditary English enemy.
Becoming good and loyal Democrats was a painless
exercise for many of Ireland's famine era arrivals.
Nonetheless, Whig leaders such as Henry Clay
believed that of all foreigners, "none amalgamate
themselves so quickly with our people as the natives
of the Emerald Isle."[43] The Irish had commenced their
political career in New York as pawns of the
Democratic Party machine. They were initially not
embraced by their chosen party. Their native-born
political acumen, however, quickly facilitated learning
the game of bartering votes to politicians in exchange
for unskilled jobs, petty licenses, and other low-cost
benefits.

These scraps represented all that the newly
impoverished newcomers could expect. As the Irish
grew in numbers and confidence, they began
collectively to make known to the organization that
such scant and ungrateful rewards for party loyalty
and support would no longer do. Becoming more
economically affluent and mobile, demands increased
with the corresponding rise in stature. By 1844, party
rolls showed the Irish were Democratic by a ratio of
95 to 5.

At first, the Democratic Party welcomed the Irish
as allies; cynically perhaps, but welcoming nonetheless. The Whigs, chafing under the failure to woo,
successfully, Irish votes, bitterly called for measures
to require a twenty-one year residency before a person
could be naturalized. William Seward was an exception. As Whig governor, he consistently advocated
support for funding of Catholic schools, a measure
that was hotly opposed by the legislature, and in later

years, would be the basis for accusations against Hughes that he was an agent of Seward and Thurlow Weed, in exchange for their doing Hughes's bidding on Catholic issues. In a ridiculously staged attempt to garner Irish support for General Winfield Scott, the Whig Presidential candidate in the Election of 1852, Irishmen were planted at a speaking stop for Scott as he unconvincingly gave his assurance to the crowd as to how much he enjoyed the sound of hearing Irish brogues. The tactic failed miserably, and the reality simply was that the Irish saw nothing of benefit in the Whig program. As Ohio Senator Tom Corwin despondently wrote about the Election of 1852, "We know they *all* {the Irish} voted the other ticket."[44]

IV

From the 1830s on, the Irish vote was being sought out in earnest. In politics, just as religion, the Irish brought to their adapted land communal traits from the old country. As the Irish became re-assimilated into Catholicism through contact with Church, parish, benevolent organization, and school, they sharpened inbred characteristics for the battle against the political advantage of the native oppressor. The success of Irish political activity in places like New York was, to a large measure, attributable to a combination of American urban machine politics with features of 19th century rural Ireland. While the Irish did not invent the "machine politics" common to America of the mid to late 1800s, their communal experience in the homeland, reinforced by the highly disciplined religious experience of the new Catholicism in their adopted land, produced eventual control over American urban politics that was nothing short of remarkable. At the height of the Repeal and Temperance movements in Ireland, Alexis de Tocqveville was struck by the powerful unity of outlook between the clergy and ordinary people. After the Cullen reforms took hold, travelers to Ireland were amazed at the increased influence that the clergy had on life generally. This reality merits a much closer look when one understands the intensely conservative and communal aspects of rural life in Ireland before the famine era.

Decisions were typically made by family councils or *clachan* committees. Lack of conformity was quickly suppressed. There was one possible explanation for why the Irish were obedient as voters to the wishes of their political, and more so, with their religious leaders. Having come from a land where oppression and coercion was a normal part of life, it was not unusual that the Irish would have aspired to, and in time, become the "regulators" in their adopted country. In a cartoon of the 1880s, long after the Irish had established themselves in their new environment, a newspaper cartoon derisively depicted a carnival booth displaying the "last non-Irish policeman in America," and even to the present day, Irish Catholics still dominate many law enforcement agencies throughout the United States.[45]

Stuffing ballot boxes or stealing elections was, to the average Irishman, less a hanging offence than a mere act of blackguarding. If anything, this behavior was carried over from the brand of corrupt political practices that characterized English administration and politics in 18th and 19th century Ireland, with the reaping of emoluments and the bartering and selling of titles and position as commonplace as the sale of horses between two gentlemen.[46]

Because of their long history in dispensing with things connected to English law that simply made no sense, the Irish developed a survival tactic with the English oppressor's administrators that reflected an innovative touch; it was the "personal" concept of how government should operate. To a countryman in Ireland, a favor given was a favor reciprocated. It was not unusual to bestow upon a local magistrate or officers of the court presents of farm produce. This gave rise to the belief that by doing a man a favor, he would be glad to do one for you, a notion which the Irish brought to perfection in the arena of New York machine politics. In countless public houses throughout Irish communities in New York and across the nation, Irishmen would vigorously recreate the concept of favor given and favor reciprocated for helping fellow immigrants in finding jobs, getting medical care, help for groceries and help in getting someone out of jail. These benefits would be rendered in exchange for political support and votes. To the Irish, influence given or gained meant a "personal relationship."[47]

The Irish brought to America another tradition of regarding the formal government as illegitimate. The Penal Laws had destroyed Catholicism, and Irish Catholics became slaves in their own country. The system made a majority population virtual outlaws in their own land, a target of contempt by the upper classes and the avowed enemies of an imposed and alien political establishment.[48]

Under these conditions, distrust of the law and distrust of the ministers and officials of state was something bred into the bones and blood of the Irish peasantry, and since the law provided them with no justice, they instituted their own. Secret societies became widespread during the Penal period, and dissimulation became a moral necessity and evasion of the law the duty of every God-fearing Catholic. This habit of mind pervaded Tammany Hall at its height, one which Hughes strongly admonished his flock to steer clear of. In a strongly worded Pastoral letter in 1842 on *Administration of the Sacraments, Secret Societies and Church Property, etc.*, Hughes eviscerated secret societies while exhorting his flock to focus on the Church and "Christ The Redeemer" himself as the universal polestar for all the good man can achieve in the world:

> "Another subject to which our attention has been directed is the existence and evils of certain societies, constituted on principles not recognized or approved by the Church. They are generally designated as 'Secret Societies,' and have, for the most part, have some professed objective of benevolence, which is used as an inducement to engage new members, and to recommend such associations to public favor. Now the members of the Catholic Church ought to know that it is not lawful for them to engage in membership of any association, not consistent with their duties as members of that great Universal Society, founded by our Redeemer, known as the Church, and which embraces all of the good that man is capable of accomplishing in this world."[49]

A band of Philadelphia nativists, fresh from a rampage of marauding and house burning, were to be welcomed with a public procession, courtesy of their sympathizers in New York City. It was in this most trying and blatant excursion into the black hole of anti-Catholicism that Hughes struck a course of moderation, patience, and sternness in the provocation of his community, sternly holding his own to the proposition that discretion was the better part of valor. This was not the first time that Catholics of New York had assumed a firm but non-violent stand against the anti-Popery faction.

Shortly after nativist activity in Boston prompted the burning of a convent in that town, an attempt was made to repeat the same act of villainy against St. Patrick's in New York. Hughes responded in the affirmative to provide for the defense of his Church. The street was torn up outside the building, and every window was made ready so that missiles could he hurled upon the attackers. The churchyard wall, though rudely constructed, was lined with men bearing muskets, many of whom belonged to the Ancient Order of Hibernians, a Catholic religious organization that had been founded in Ireland in the 1500s for the avowed purpose of protecting the Mass, Priest, and the Catholic Church. The would-be attackers, realizing that those within the campus were men fully prepared to fight to the last in defense of their altar and their faith, dispersed and prevented what would have certainly been fatal bloodshed on both sides.

A meeting of New York Native Americans was called in City Hall Park. The purpose of this meeting was to give a "suitable" reception to the marauders of Philadelphia. Bishop Hughes made it clear through the *Freeman's Journal* that the scenes of Philadelphia would not be renewed with impunity in New York, and was known to have said in reply to a priest who had seen the conflagration in Philadelphia and, who was advising Hughes to publish an address urging Catholics to keep the peace, "If a single Catholic

Church," said Hughes, "was burned in New York City, the city would become a second Moscow."[50] Again, through the *Freeman*, the bishop sternly cautioned the Irish to stay away from the public meetings, especially the one to be held in the Park. It cannot be overstated that a weak leader at a time of such a poisoned atmosphere of hatred around his followers could not have made as disciplined, determined, and effective response to such a threat.

That the Irish were prepared to fight their Protestant nativist tormentors with a vengeance is without question. There was no difference in the face of the foe, whether it be Vinegar Hill in Wexford or the ramshackle, filthy streets of Sweeney's Shambles. While the Catholic churches of New York were sufficiently defended by a force of men resolved to die if necessary in their defense, it was only the steely and unswerving determination of Hughes that ultimately prevented the kind of unbridled violence that had swept Philadelphia, Boston, and St. Louis to take root in New York. In an extraordinary interview with New York's Democratic Mayor, Robert Hunter Morris, Hughes, though not stated in tones of belligerency, nonetheless conveyed a sense of unmistakable consequences if city authorities failed to recognize the emergency and take appropriate action. That the Roman Catholic Bishop of New York, as head of a minority and intensely persecuted religion, could psychologically reverse roles with the principal elected official of the city, speaks volumes of the moral supremacy of a man unhesitatingly prepared to deal with foes. It was the words unsaid by Hughes that made it evident to Mayor Morris that the nativist partisans of hatred had much to lose:

"Are you afraid," asked the Mayor, "that some of your churches will be burned?"

"No sir," replied Hughes, "but I am afraid that some of yours will be burned. We can protect our own. I came to warn you for your own good."

"Do you think, Bishop, that your people would attack the procession?"

"I do not, but the Native Americans want to provoke a Catholic riot, and if they can do it in no other way, I believe they would not scruple to attack the procession themselves, for the sake of making it appear that the Catholics had assailed them."

"What, then, would you have me do?"

"I did not come here to tell you what to do. I am a churchman, not the Mayor of New York; but if I were the Mayor, I would examine the laws of the state, and see if there were not attached to the police force a battery of artillery, a company or so of infantry, and a squadron of horses; and I think I should find that if there were, and if so, I should call them out. Moreover, I should send to Mr. Harper, the Mayor-elect, who has been chosen by the votes of this party. I should remind him that these men are his supporters; I should warn him that if they carry out their design, there will be a riot; and I urge him to use his influence in preventing his public reception of the delegates."[51]

As mayor, Morris clearly had an obligation to consider the safety of all of New York's citizens. As a young man, he had attended the Washington Bible

Seminary and clearly was possessed of the establishment's nativist sympathies. There was, however, no escaping the determined Hughes, a man who Morris perceived at that moment to be in possession of the keys to continued peace and calm in the city of New York. A fearful and indecisive person may have lost the discipline needed at that moment to stand up to the prospect of his people coming under such potential violent attack with virtually no recourse in law. Even though Hughes was at a great disadvantage, his even tempered approach and the brilliant step taken of coming to "warn" the chief elected official of New York of the consequences for failure to act had its telling effect. There was no public demonstration, and in the end, the course taken by Hughes in admonishing his people as he did, spared a city bloodshed, pillage, murder, and the internecine hatred of Christian using club and gun against Christian.

V

Hughes was the quintessential American nationalist. He preached to his people a gospel that incorporated love of the Church, love of America, and love of the Irish homeland. He ardently supported the war against Mexico (1846-47), though it was a war against a Catholic country. Hughes supported the administration of James K. Polk, even though the war pitted Irish immigrants against their Mexican coreligionists in battle and to carry out the conquest of towns where women and children huddled together and prayed in Catholic churches for protection against the enemy. Yet within the United States Army of the time, the presence of Catholic priests was forbidden, and

Catholic soldiers were compelled to attend Protestant services. While Polk's Whig opponents railed against a conflict whose true purpose they believed to be land grabbing, the same racist assumptions and prejudices made about Mexicans had found ample sustenance from within the vile feed bag that nativists had characterized the famine Irish. This sentiment was most succinctly summarized by Captain William S. Henry, posted in the disputed area between Mexico and the United States along the Rio Grande: "It certainly was never intended that this lovely land should remain in the hands of an ignorant and degenerate race."[52]

The Mexican government, not unaware of the intensive anti-Catholic bigotry that existed in the United States, offered land to Catholic immigrants who would desert and take up the war against the American enemy. Upwards of 25% of those serving in the army of General Zachary Taylor were Irish Immigrants. They suffered the same treatment of their co-religionists who remained at home, for the army officer corps of the period was largely Protestant, largely nativist in sentiment, and largely ill disposed to the Irish. President Polk, however, recognized the tremendous influence and power of Hughes, and offered to send Hughes to Mexico as a minister, a position he turned down because of its unofficial nature:

> "Bishop Hughes called with Mr. Buchanan at seven o'clock. Mr. Buchanan, having already conversed with me on the subject, retired, and I held a conversation for an hour with him. I fully explained to him the objections which we would probably encounter from the prejudices of the Catholic priests in Mexico

and that our object was not to overthrow their religion and rob their churches. Bishop Hughes fully agreed with me in the opinion that it was important to remove such impressions. I said to him that it was the great object of my desiring to have this interview with him to ask whether some of the priests of the United States who spoke the Spanish language could be induced to accompany our army as chaplains. Bishop Hughes at once said that having a few Catholic priests with the army would have a good effect, and expressed his entire willingness to cooperate with the government in giving such aid as was within his power. I found Bishop Hughes a highly intelligent and agreeable man, and my interview with him was of the most satisfactory character."[53]

Polk's supposed offer of a post to Hughes, however, did not escape the wrath of Protestant critics. Enraged at the prospect of sending Hughes in any official capacity on behalf of the government, the *Church Times*, a religious publication of the Baltimore Presbyterians, editorialized in unabashed, irate terms concerning the rumor of such an appointment: "...A Presbyterian President calls upon a Roman Bishop to give assistance in a state affair. Mr. Polk has involved his country in a war, and notwithstanding the great horror which men of his stamp feel of the encroachments of Rome, he does not scruple to give her a pretense for interference even at the center of government, by soliciting her good offices to protect the American army from anticipated foes...We shall see the end when the end comes. But meanwhile, it may be interesting for observers of the times to watch the course of the incipient court paid by the state to the Church of Rome."[54]

In similar fashion were editorials in anti-Catholic publications such as *The Herald*, loath in their belief that Hughes was to be sent to Mexico. One such article, appearing in the *New York Daily Tribune*, set about creating an atmosphere of conspiratorial intrigue between President Polk and Hughes:

> "We have received intelligence from an authentic source at Washington that negotiations of a perfectly astounding character are in progress between the Right Rev. John Hughes, Bishop of New York, and the President of the United States. We have the particulars before us and will probably publish them in a few days when we get a fuller and more detailed account. This affair, when published, will be far more interesting and create greater excitement among all classes, and more especially among the anti-Catholic portion of the community, than even the awful disclosures of Maria Monk or any other awful disclosures that have been published for the last fifty years. This new and extraordinary move of Bishop Hughes will cause a good deal of astonishment."[55]

In reality, little information about the subject was ever forthcoming from Hughes himself. In discussing the interview with intimates, he never revealed the entire story because he felt it would have been wholly inappropriate to discuss what had transpired in conversation between himself and the President of the United States. While obviously gratified in the great confidence reposed in his talents, Hughes had neither the ambition nor the desire to go to Mexico. "As a citizen of the United States, I am bound to serve my country with all of the energies I possess; and as a Christian Bishop, I am bound to be a messenger of peace; but I have no favors to ask from any, and I have important objects to fill at home."[56]

By 1847, Hughes was approaching a pinnacle of power and influence hitherto inconceivable for a member of the Catholic clergy. He was perfectly at ease among the most notable statesman of the period and was on friendly terms with many of them. When Henry Clay visited New York City, Hughes and his secretary called upon him at his hotel where Clay, obviously delighted by the unexpected honor, sat in a conversation with the prelate for over an hour.

The esteem of Hughes was no more greatly manifested than by invitation to preach to the members of the United States Congress. The invitation arrived and thus addressed to the prelate as follows:

> "Sir, the undersigned members of Congress respectfully invite you to preach in the Hall of the House of Representatives on Sunday next (12th inst.) at 11 o'clock, unless some other hour of the day may be more agreeable to you....
>
> We are, Right Rev. Sir, your obedient servants."

The invitation included the names of some twenty members of the Senate and thirty-three members of the House of Representatives. On December 9th, Speaker of the House, Robert C. Winthrop, added the following addendum to the previously issued invite:

"It gives me great pleasure to place the Hall of
the House of the Representatives at the
service of Bishop Hughes, in conformity with
the above invitation."[57]

While the list of signatories to the invitation was
not as large as it would have been had the other
members of the body been able to respond generally,
it did, however, have the names of the leading men of
both parties in Congress. In his acceptance of the
invitation, Hughes, in his reply, stated that, "I do not
feel at liberty to decline a compliance with a wish so
kindly expressed on your part and so flattering to me.
I have the honor to remain, gentleman, Your Obedient
Servant, John Hughes, Bishop of New York."[58]

Hughes preached Americanism and the virtues
associated with good citizenship. It was a charge
constantly hurled by the enemy against Irish Catholics; that is, they were incapable of truly learning and
practicing the democratic virtues of the republic, and
utterly incapable of meaningful political discourse
because of their allegiance to the Pope. And so on the
day of his epochal sermon before the Congress of the
United States, delivered on Sunday, December 12th,
1847, it was only fitting that the topic of the sermon
was "Christianity," the only source of moral, social,
and political regeneration. In his concluding remarks,
Hughes appropriately proclaimed that, "If a man
would serve his country, his fellow men, if he would
procure to himself the highest enjoyment of which his
own nature is capable, he will be more studious of the
comforts, rights, and interests of others than his
own."[59] This sentiment also reflected something
unspoken in connection to his own immigrant flock...
a hope that his people would one day be accepted

fully as members of a country destined to be a beacon
light of the world:

> "...and now I would breathe a prayer to God,
> that he will preserve you [Congress], and that
> you, above all, to whom the nation and the
> world look with so much confidence, may be
> guided in your deliberations by the Spirit of
> God; that you may be enlightened where light
> is necessary, and swayed in your judgment in
> favor of those decisions which will at once
> promote the glory of our common Father, and
> the interests of this great and growing
> country, whose destinies may exercise here-
> after so important an influence upon the
> nations of the earth."[60]

As Hughes grew in stature beyond his Diocesan
See, his flock was also growing in great numbers. By
virtue of the steady influx of Irish fleeing the famine,
the Catholic Church of New York would experience
exponential growth from the period between 1846 and
1851, when an estimated one million persons made
the voyage across the ocean from Ireland. Protestants
were being swamped by the rapidly advancing numbers of foreigners. The numbers of Irish Catholics
from the standpoint of political strength was not lost
on the nativists. Just as during the Public School
Society controversy earlier on, Protestant Americans
now more than ever feared the threatening influence
of Irish Catholics, who were now sufficiently overcoming the initial shock of immigration to impact the
political and social landscape. A generation prior, this
would have been inconceivable. More intensely feared
and hated was the mechanism that had spawned the

emergence of the Irish, that being their Church and its most vocal and recognized leader.

In 1850, the New York Diocese was raised to the status of an Archdiocese, and consequently, Hughes was named its first Archbishop on October 3rd. For over a decade, he had fought the abject hatred of nativism, built up a remote and scattered diocese with schools, orphanages, and benevolent institutions, and oversaw the increase in Catholic Clergy and religious orders to service the needs of the burgeoning Catholic population, but most importantly, reintroduced and tirelessly worked to turn the pitiless masses of famine Irish immigrants from an impoverished rabble into a churched, more pietistic and devotionally attuned Catholic community. In hand with the former, Hughes fostered among his countryman a devotion for the United States, the virtues of good and sober living, and involvement in the political process for the furtherance of good to be attained for them and their posterity.

As the Irish population swelled in the mid-19th century, there were hardly enough churches to serve the needs of the people. No church more epitomized the commitment of Hughes to insure that his people did not languish in spiritual poverty than the church of St. Brigid. In 1848, he ordered Father Kein to build a parish for the Irish near Tompkins Square. Kein bought a piece of land at Avenue B and 8th Street. The church was to be dedicated to St. Brigid, "the virgin saint of Erin," who heard St. Patrick himself preach. The cornerstone of the church was laid by Hughes on September 10th, 1848, and so big was the crowd for the dedication that the walls people sat on to get a better view of the ceremonies literally sank under the massive weight. The building was ready for its first Mass on Sunday, December 2, 1849. Great

credit for the speedy erection of the church went to
Patrick Keely, an Irish immigrant at the start of a
brilliant career that was to make him out as one of
the most successful and popular builders of Catholic
Churches in 19th century America. At a time when
church finances were extremely limited and the
services of architects recklessly extravagant, Keely
was able to produce designs that were both within
budget and on time. When he died in 1896, over 600
churches stretching from Canada to Mexico had been
built by him.

St. Brigid's parish was typical of the Catholic
parishes of the era; that is, it was strapped for cash.
The parish residents were poor and contributed what
little they could, but pastors struggled to keep the
parish afloat financially. The idea of working class
Catholics contributing monies to create a magnificent
church building was far from reflective of the reality:
much of the Irish immigrant community was still
living a state of acute economic distress.[61] Still, slowly
but steadily, the Irish Catholic community, even
though the initial phase of extreme material poverty
and spiritual dearth had been a hard bitten reality in
their new surroundings, a community began to
emerge from the trauma of immigration that was
beginning to gain more confidence in its own direction
and self-sufficiency. There were yet many harsh
obstacles to overcome and much prejudice and
hostility to endure, but by the start of the middle
decade of the 19th century, Irish Catholics were
clearly on the rise. As well, in the decade to come,
Hughes would emerge a true national figure, a friend,
and confident of William Seward and the powerful
New York political boss, Thurlow Weed. Ultimately,
these liaisons would bring him into the orbit of
Abraham Lincoln, the tall, brooding, and rumpled

one-term Congressman and defeated Senate candidate from Illinois, who would, in the momentous Presidential campaign of 1860, be elected the 16th President of the United States and lead the nation through four years of bitter and bloody civil war. Irish Catholics in the thousands would take up arms for the preservation of that same nation, proving their loyalty in the spilling of blood in combat.

Chapter 4

"I Know Nothing"

The decade of the 1850s dawned with the sectional differences between North and South growing more acute. The issue of slavery was intensifying these differences, and southern sensibilities with respect to an acknowledgement of southern rights concerning the "peculiar institution" was meeting more and more with an inflexible response from Abolitionist sentiment in the North. Hughes himself was an avid anti-Abolitionist. He detested Abolitionism as an extreme position because he believed that the immediate freeing of Black slaves would be harmful to them. More directly, Hughes objected to the Abolitionist position because of its hypocrisy; that is, many who simultaneously espoused freedom for the Blacks were rabid anti-immigrant and anti-Catholic proponents as well. Additionally, masses of freed slaves would represent economic competition for his own people, who were at the very bottom of the ladder in terms of employment prospects and income.[1]

In view of these circumstances, the allegations often raised by militant Protestants that Hughes was pro-secession and anti-Union gave further life to the notion that his legions of Irish Catholic dirt farmers could neither be trusted nor were capable of ever becoming good and loyal Americans...Americans who would give allegiance to the President of the United States rather than the Pope. For Hughes's enemies, it had always been too convenient to cast this cleric of ever-growing influence in opposition to things American, such as during the intensely partisan school debate and the establishment of separate Catholic schools. Allegiance of Irish Catholics had fiercely been to their Church and not the high-minded republican institutions tenaciously defended by mainline American Protestantism. This may have been true in the early stages of the famine Irish settlement, but by the time of the Civil War, the pro-Americanism Hughes had always preached was now preeminent in the establishment of Hughes as an arch defender of the Union and the Constitution. He was not in any sense a personal supporter of slavery, for as a Roman Catholic, he had been born into slavery in his native Ireland, and knew well the degradation and humiliation accompanying servitude and the absence of freedom. Whatever sympathies Hughes may have had with the South lay in the fact that his antagonism toward Abolitionism and Abolitionists won esteem for the Catholic Church in pro-slavery circles, a reality that minimized nativist opposition to Catholics and their Church in the South.

On the other hand, members of the Catholic clergy, consistent with centuries of Catholic tradition, were slave holders themselves in many cases, and while they advocated the humane treatment of slaves and insisted that blacks were human beings entitled to religious education, the benefits of religion, family life, and decent food and shelter, they never agitated for an end to slavery.[2] Hughes and Catholics generally saw abolitionism as a direct challenge to the

Constitutional guarantee of a man's right to his property; that is, the right to have and keep slaves where the institution already existed. To Hughes, as well as to many Catholics, North and South was the acknowledgement that slavery was an issue of States Rights, the domain where the issue of slavery resided and should remain. Scripture and Catholic tradition affirmed its legitimacy.

The decade of the 1850s also marked the establishment of New York as an Archdiocesan See and the elevation of Hughes to an Archbishop. His Irish community was vastly growing in size and, consequently, growing in the disdain of nativists, who feared their eventual drowning in the surging waters of "Popery." In the poisoned atmosphere of the Know-Nothing campaign, some Irish Catholic editors started appealing to people in Ireland to make Canada their destination for emigrating rather than the United States; however, "the remittances from this country have much more weight than abusive editorials, and they fear less the denunciation of the clergy than they do to lose the chance to share with those relatives here the blessings of freedom and the chance of becoming what, in Ireland, under existing circumstances, they could not become."[3] The Irish in New York and elsewhere were here to stay, and no amount of nativist intimidation or violence would deter them. "The Catholic papers have, with a surprising unanimity, frowned on the proposition of peopling Canada with the Irish emigration. It is but moving from one province of Great Britain to another."[4]

No event in New York City more greatly represented the growing confidence and pride felt by the Irish Catholic community than the St. Patrick's Day Parade, started in 1762 as a social among Irish soldiers serving in the British Army.[5] As *The New*

York Times reported, "Most extensive preparations were made for the celebration on Saturday of the anniversary of St. Patrick's Day. It was the intention of the Irish population to signalize the present anniversary of the birth of their patron saint with a degree of 'pomp and circumstances' of glorious display, paralleled by any previous celebration. All the Irish benevolent and kindred Irish associations were intending to join in the procession."

On the evening previous, there was a meeting at Montgomery Hall of delegates from the different societies who were to join in the procession, to agree upon the route to be taken, which was decided as follows: "to form at nine o'clock A.M. on Second Avenue, with the right resting on Eighth Street, thence to march down the avenue to Second Street, through Second Street to the Bowery, down the Bowery to Chatham Street, and from Chatham Street to the Park, where they were to pass in front of the City Hall to be reviewed by His Honor, the Mayor, and the Common Council at twelve o'clock. From there, they were to march up Broadway and Fourth Avenue to Twenty-Third Street, thence through to Second Avenue, and down to the place of starting, and there dismiss."[6]

The festive atmosphere of the day, however, did not permeate the halls of the American Protestant Association, who, responding to the editor of *The New York Times* under the heading *Irishmen that Don't Honor St. Patrick*, made their views quite clear with respect to any day honoring Ireland's patron saint: "In your paper this morning, you say, 'All the Irish benevolent and kindred Irish Associations were intending to join in the procession.' On the part of the American Protestant Association, allow me to say that the greater number of the members thereof are

Irishmen, but it never was, and never will be, their intention to join in any procession the object of which is to show reverence for the birth or death day of any man."[7] In Poughkeepsie, New York, though, in the far flung reaches of Hughes's Archdiocese and a long way from the Irish benevolent and kindred associations shoulder to shoulder on the march past City Hall, the ugly head of anti-Irish and anti-Catholic bigotry was alive and well: "An effigy with a string of potatoes round its neck, and labeled 'St. Patrick,' hung this morning on an elm tree in front of the Gregory House. No effort has been made to take it down."[8]

From the 1830s until the 1850s, outbreaks of violence against immigrant Catholics had been a normal and accepted aspect of American society. In this period, the level of anti-Catholicism from Kentucky to Maine had left both immigrant and nativists dead in the street. The level of anti-Catholicism had reached a fever pitch in American life, perhaps never before, and perhaps never again, to be seen in its intensity.

Appearing in a publication called the *American Protestant Vindicator* in January of 1841, the insidious and pervasive hatred of Roman Catholicism was captured in poetic verse:

> "Rome's true minions, chain them down,
> In ignorance from heel to crown;
> In hopes, perchance that when the
> Pope,
> Is forced from Europe to elope,
> He here may find a sovereign throne;
> And ready serfs to bend and groan."[9]

Throughout the country, assorted Protestant publications such as the *American Protestant Vindicator* and *Anti-Jesuit* railed against Popish corruption and false doctrines. Debates were organized to address questions such as "Is Popery Compatible with Civil Liberty?" Resistance to the Catholic onslaught even began taking on a more formal face during this period with the emergence of organized political parties with names like the American Republicans and the Native Americans. New York's Mayor, James Harper, who had been elected to office at the height of nativist agitation and violence in the mid 40s, had been elected as the American Republican candidate. The most famous of these groups, however, was to be known as simply the American Party, more widely known as "the Know-Nothings." The group was organized in 1849 by a New Yorker named Charles B. Allan, originally under the title of the Order of the Star Spangled Banner. Membership requirements called for being born in the United States, being born to protestant parents, and to not be married to a Roman Catholic. The group had secret signals, handshakes, and passwords. The organization's members would be asked: "Are you willing to use your influence and vote only for native-born American citizens for all offices of honor, trust, or profit in the gifts of the people, the exclusion of all foreigners, and Roman Catholics in particular, and without regard to party predilections?"[10]

I

Arriving in the United States for the purpose of bestowing Papal blessing upon the country, Gaetano Bedini, Papal Nuncio to the United States, did little more than foment rioting by nativist factions in his port city of entry, Philadelphia. His travel to the U.S.

had from the outset been ill advised by the American
hierarchy, and the civil disorders which raged in
Philadelphia upon his arrival were the proof for the
advice given for him not to visit. Further complicating
an already tense situation was Bedini's American tour
being hounded by the presence of Allesandro Gavazzi,
an ex-monk and strident Italian nationalist. At each
of Bedini's stops, Cincinnati, Baltimore, Boston, and
New York, charges by Gevazzi of Bedini's approval of
the executions of hundreds of Italian nationalists,
with the nativist press taking up the accusations in
full editorial bombast, created hysteria and violence
all along his travel route. For security reasons, the
helpless nuncio, scorned, and burned in effigy, was
smuggled aboard a ship in New York harbor to be
hustled away to safety.

A self-styled imitator of Allesandro Gevazzi,
named John C. Orr, led a campaign of violence
against the Catholic Church throughout New England
that included church burnings and the tarring and
feathering of a priest in Maine. Priests were beaten
while making their routine parish visitations. In New
York, Archbishop Hughes once again squared off with
aggressive nativist factions. In Louisville, Kentucky, at
least twenty people would die in the streets on what
was to be infamously known in that city's history as
"Bloody Monday," a day of anti-Catholic, nativist-
incited violence, incited by a nativist mayor.[11]

> "At a late hour on Wednesday night, a gang of
> lawless ruffians, the same, no doubt, who
> have been committing numerous cowardly
> and brutal excesses in the lower part of city,
> made an attack on the house of Mr. F. Quinn.
> Several of the houses were stoned and much
> defaced. A woman, Mrs. Lee, was shot

through the arm. No arrests were made. Threats of burning the property last night were uttered. A malicious rumor was started that fire-arms were concealed in the Catholic Church on Thirteenth Street, which was promptly allayed by the church doors being open by the priest in charge, and the building searched. Of course, nothing warlike was found."[12]

It was in this atmosphere that the Know-Nothing Party officially organized itself on a national basis in 1854, on a platform of straight out anti-Catholicism. Sizable electoral gains were made in many states, most notably in Massachusetts, where a solid 63% of the electorate elections voted in Know-Nothing candidates, taking all of the state senate seats and all but two seats in the assembly. A Know-Nothing candidate captured the mayoralty of Philadelphia. In Pennsylvania and New York, they captured 40% and 25% of the cast ballots respectively. In 1855, the Know-Nothings made sizable electoral inroads in the state of California and throughout the South. In the National Congressional elections of 1854, no fewer than 120 members of Congress counted themselves as members of the Know-Nothing Party. In 1856, their nominee for President was former President Millard Fillmore.[13]

For over thirty years standing in an incomplete state, the Washington Monument was perhaps the best representative piece of anti-Catholic nativist paranoia. A two-thousand-year-old inscribed stone from the Temple of Concord in the city of Rome had been sent as a gift to the United States by the Pope in honor of the monument being constructed to honor America's first President. A nativist rumor spread to the effect that the arrival of the stone and completion of the monument was to signal the start of a Catholic uprising. As a result, a band of men stole the stone and threw it into the Potomac River on the night of March 26th, 1854. The following day, a Know-Nothing faction took control of the monument project. Owing to the volatile nature of the incident, Congress failed to provide additional funding for completion of the monument. The unfinished monument was to stand for three decades as the stark and bitter reminder of furtive Protestant bigotry and intolerance.[14]

The feeling of nativist superiority and unbridled racist contempt for the Catholic Irish is so vividly captured in the diary of George Templeton Strong, who writing in 1848 at the time of him building a house, recorded:

> "Hibernia came to the rescue yesterday morning; twenty 'sons of toil' with prehensible paws supplied them by nature with evident reference to the handling of the spade and the wielding of the pickaxe and congenital hollows on the shoulders wonderfully adapted to make the carrying of the hod a luxury instead of a labor. This is an English colony [with] the true Saxon contempt for everything Irish."[15]

II

In the bitter public school issue, Hughes had become an ally of then New York Governor William H. Seward. The public school issue forged an alliance between the usually pro-Democratic Catholic Church and the usually anti-immigrant Whig Party. The perception of

Hughes as a raw politician gained momentum during this period, as he was believed to be an agent of the Seward-Weed faction, doing their bidding, in exchange for their support of Catholic interests.

In an article appearing in the *Albany State Register* entitled *Another Long Bull from the Vatican*, published by the editor, S.H. Hammond, hostile and bigoted in content, Hammond attempted to castigate Hughes and his Church's alleged meddling in the political process. The controversy this time whirled around proposed legislation in the New York State Assembly that would have allowed congregations to own church property rather than in the name of the religious organization of which it was a part. This legislation was clearly anti-Catholic, and Erastus Brooks, a Know-Nothing leader, had made a powerful speech on the floor of the state Senate on March 6th, 1855, charging Hughes with being the holder of four or five millions of Church property. Hughes, in his position as Archbishop, as was the case throughout the Catholic diocesan system, was holder of the property endowed to the institutional Catholic Church. He, of course, became the obvious target, depicted and vilified as a medieval prince, whose people were mere serfs, incapable of being loyal to none other than the Pope. Hughes, in his opening retort to Hammond, states: "Mr. Hammond has insinuated another charge to which I think it proper that I should make a suitable reply. He assumes them as matters not to be called into question. He passes from the Catholic individual to the Catholic system, and betrays unmistakable evidences that, whether artificially or naturally, he is under the influence of an anti-Popery mania."[16]

Hughes was answering to the accusation of Hammond that, because Governor Seward had

intimated that Hughes was a friend, the relationship
was one in which political preference in favor of
Catholic issues, and the ultimate control and introduction of Catholic policy in the political process,
would find a conduit for expression:

> "If the Catholic religion forms alliances with
> political ambition, and joins hands with the
> demagogues of party, Mr. Hammond is more
> guilty than those he accuses, if he conceals
> the facts which would substantiate his
> assertion. If, as he says, Gov. Seward did me
> the favor of calling me his friend, and to say
> he respected and confided in me, it is more
> than I ever knew or heard before; but as to
> the confidence reposed in me, Governor
> Seward would not have been disappointed.
> Mr. Hammond has said that Governor Seward
> was then speaking of a political friend and
> associate; and I can assure him that in this
> statement, he has forsaken the path of truth.
> This I know of my own knowledge. I am not a
> political friend and associate of Governor
> Seward; I never was; I am not his confederate
> in securing political influence. I am not his
> supporter in the exercise of power. And yet I
> am proud to call him my friend, in the only
> relation that ever existed between us, which
> has been one of mere social, and to me,
> pleasant intercourse. If the people of the
> United States should think proper to confer
> upon him the highest honor in their gift, I
> shall not heave a sigh or shed a tear at their
> choice. But no vote of mine shall aid him. In
> this, as in all his public acts, he is in the
> hands of his countrymen; and I am well

dispensed from the necessity of either approving or condemning his principles or his conduct."[17]

Hughes's reply had the usual effect of his responses to attacks of this nature, namely, broadening the scope of the conflict at hand, which, in this instance, appears to have played well in augmenting the Know-Nothing agitation that Senator Brooks so well represented. As George Templeton Strong noted in a diary entry of November 7th, 1855: "Erastus Brooks triumphantly re-elected to the State Senate from the Sixth district, a cruel blow to Archbishop Hughes. I wonder if it is true that he received a large silent Irish Catholic vote?"[18]

But Hughes had meddled in the process, more out of necessity in the face of the unfair and inequitable legislative campaign against the Petitioners for a share of obtaining money for Catholic schools during the public school debate back in the early 1840s. On this point, Hughes reminded Hammond, who was obviously not of an age to remember the funding controversy, of the circumstances under which proactive interference was of paramount importance for his people: "To affect the change, we had to appeal by petition to the Legislature of the State, where petition was denied; next, to the Legislature of the State, where the change took place not precisely as we would have desired, but as the Legislature thought proper to make it. Mr. Hammond will be pleased to take particular notice of the fact that I am now about to mention that within a few days of the election, the Public School Society, by their agents, waited on the candidates of the Legislature, and required a pledge from them, from those of one party as well those of the another, to refuse the petition for a change in the system of education, in the event of their being elected. This was too much. It was secret. It was insidious. It left Catholics to vote for one party or the other, concealing from them that no matter which party they voted for, or which candidate, they were elevating into power men who has prejudged their cause, and had bound themselves to reject even a consideration of its merits."

Hughes pointedly closed in the admission to Hammond that he had meddled: "I urged them [The Petitioners], with all of the zeal and earnestness I was capable of, to refuse the vote of any man of any party, who has accepted the degrading pledge, that if elected, he would refuse them even the chance of obtaining justice. If this was meddling in politics, then I did meddle once, but I have never regretted it. On the contrary, there is nothing in my life, apart from my sacred ministry, to which I took back with so much satisfaction as to the course I pursued on that occasion."[19]

The question of Hughes's suspected attempt to subvert the political process in the name of Catholic issues very much was indicative of the still pervasive and nagging question in the minds of nativists; that is, could Catholics, and by implication, "the Irish," be loyal and faithful to these ideals of the American way of life? The property issue had forced the other Catholic bishops to take their cue from New York. The strong trustee bill that was being pushed in the New York State legislature was quietly repealed in 1863. In the intervening period, Hughes simply ignored it. In furtherance of Protestant concern about Catholic proselytizing, Hughes gave his opponents one further rub and more reason to worry:

"Roman Catholicism will convert all Pagan nations and all Protestant nations, even England with her proud Parliament. Everybody should know that we have our mission to convert the world, including the inhabitants of the United States, the people of the cities, and the people of the country, the officers of the Navy and the Marines, commander of the Army, the legislatures, the Senate, the Cabinet, the President, and all."[20]

At a time when political tempers were growing ever shorter over the contentious slavery issue, the prospect of armed conflict between the North and South was gaining a momentum that within a few short years was to tragically explode in bloody civil war. Who, wondered the established order, were these Irish to serve...priest or patria?

III

By the mid-19th century, the issue of slavery had come to dominate the political agenda of the nation. The slavery issue was becoming intertwined with issue of Irish nationalism. Petitions flooded the halls of Congress to bring pressure to bear on the British to free the Irish political prisoners associated with that nation's failed uprising in 1848. Southern senators vehemently objected to the proposal on the grounds that Irish freedom could translate into freedom for slaves.[21] The point became moot when John Mitchel and others who had been imprisoned in the English Penal colony in Van Dieman's Land (Tasmania) arrived in New York in November of 1853 to a warm and enthusiastic reception at City Hall. Mitchel's decorum and pronouncements worked to alienate him from the people to whom he sought recognition as a leader. He incorrectly believed that the accolades showered upon him were not meant for him personally, but as direct insults to the English government. He greatly criticized Secretary of State William Marcy and American foreign policy at a banquet, proclaiming himself a "professed revolutionist," who wanted the United States to become a stamping ground for revolution. He further antagonized potential supporters by stating that he found no crime in slavery. "We, for our part," stated Mitchel, "wish we had a good plantation, well stocked with healthy negroes in Alabama."[22] For many New Yorkers, including Horace Greeley, editor of the *Tribune*, this statement obliterated any support for the cause of Irish freedom.

Next, and most disastrously, Mitchel offended Archbishop Hughes by supporting the seizure of Rome by Italian Republicans and their creation of a new civil government. This was anathema to Hughes, who had always preached unequivocally about the legitimacy of the Pope's temporal power. While Hughes had been an ardent supporter of Catholic Emancipation and had met and greatly admired Daniel O'Connell, he did not believe that his flock should give their support to Irish revolutionary movements in Ireland that had little prospect of success, save for a few brief moments of recognition. On the contrary, he continued to preach and instill a consistent and steady path toward achieving freedom by support of the American way of life, culture, and laws.

Slavery remained a contentious issue, and a statement by Daniel O'Connell and a Papal Bull from Pope Gregory the XVI, both condemning the "peculiar institution," many, including the *Citizen* founded by

Mitchel in 1854, thought it was a "bad Irishman" who would jeopardize the present freedom of a nation of white men for the vague forlorn hope of elevating blacks.[23]

Like the anti-masonic party before, the Know-Nothings transformed themselves from a group of local voluntary associations into a nationwide political party to obtain their objectives, which included severe limits on immigration from Catholic countries; restricting of office to native-born Americans of English and Scotch Protestant lineage only; mandating a 21 year wait until immigrants could gain citizenship; restricting of public school teaching positions to Protestants only; mandating daily Bible readings in public schools; restricting the sale of liquor and restricting the use of languages other than English. The political parties of the time printed their own ballots, and then tried to persuade voters to cast them. In the North, the nativist American party probably polled as many votes as the Democrats and Whigs. Overall, the Know-Nothing movement ultimately did more harm to the Whigs than to its rival Democratic Party. The Irish voted overwhelmingly for the pro-immigrant Democrats. Because of the Roman Catholic Church's silence on the issue of slavery, abolitionists felt sympathy with nativism, while others like William Seward disassociated himself from it. The leaders of both major political parties agreed in their condemnation of nativism because it represented a threat to both. Such apprehensions were justified, because Know-Nothingism made great gains both locally and nationally in the Presidential election of 1852 and Congressional elections of 1854.

Hughes, always primed for the brawling style of battle he savored, again became involved in a bitterly acrimonious conflict with James Gordon Bennett, owner of the *New York Herald*. As the Know-Nothing sentiment grew, Bennett's paper was a major conduit for the dissemination of anti-Irish, anti-Catholic, and generally anti-immigrant commentary. Bennett was intensely American in all of his attitudes, which became a preponderant factor in his paper's influence abroad. Hughes, knowing that Bennett was a Catholic, presumed to use this fact in his dealings with the mercurial newspaperman, which proved to be a mistake. Although baptized and married in the Catholic Church, Bennett resented the mastery of the Church and stated so plainly. It is possible that the antipathy he felt in this regard stemmed from the experience of his brother Cosmo, who died as the result of the rigorous asceticism that was part of the training he underwent to become a priest in his youth.

Hughes fulminated and thundered against Bennett from the pulpit of St. Patrick's with the furious and frenzied back and forth between the two antagonists facilitated by rival editors who printed Hughes's recriminations. These attacks ultimately helped the *Herald*, but then Hughes responded by excommunicating Bennett. Continuing his crusade, Bennett called for a complete separation of the American Catholic Church from control of the rule of Rome. He argued for and demanded an American church free of the control of the hierarchy.[24]

Bennett, however, was to fire the final salvo, and determined that the Archbishop was not to go unscathed in this engagement, summed up Hughes's activities to date in the following acerbic manner:

"The conduct of the bishop in 1841 gave preponderance to the Irish in 1842, which in turn created a reaction in the American mind in 1843, resulting in the organization of the Native American Party last spring, and whose operations we have all seen. But all these movements, here as in Philadelphia, can be traced, with the accuracy of mathematical calculation, back to Bishop Hughes's first entrance into Carroll Hall as a political agitator, and the motives which impelled the Bishop then can be guessed at now with a good deal of certainty. He was the first dignitary of the Catholic Church, in this free and happy land, that ever attempted such a movement, and we trust that he may be the last of the same faith that may ever thus disgrace his holy calling. In all these movements, he has most woefully mistaken his duties. He has woefully mistaken his position in this city, in this country, and in this age. He has forgotten that he is living in a land of freedom and universal toleration, in a republic of intelligent men, and in the 19th century."[25]

The power of the Native American movement as a political force was destined, however, to be short lived. After 1855, the party began to decline in the North. In the Presidential election of 1856, the party was bitterly divided over the all-consuming issue of slavery. The main faction within the movement supported the ticket of Millard Fillmore, a Whig who had served as the 13th President of the United States, and his Vice-Presidential running mate, Andrew Jackson Donelson, who was the nephew of former Democratic President, Andrew Jackson, 7th President of the United States.

This ticket was designed to appeal to loyalists from both the Democratic and Whig parties. They won 23% of the popular vote and captured the eight electoral votes of one...Maryland. The nativist platform and appeal, even with Fillmore and Jackson as the standard bearers, was not enough to keep the White House from going to the Democrat, James Buchanan.

After the Supreme Court's decision in the Dred Scott Case in 1857, most of the anti-slavery members of the American Party joined the newly formed Republican Party (modern day Republican Party). In the south, the American Party's pro-slavery wing remained, for a short time, strong on the state and local level, but by 1860, had virtually ceased to be a serious national political movement.[26]

The rise of the Know-Nothings and accompanying political movement coincided with an end in the 1850s of the first major wave of immigrants to America's shores, who were not of so-called Anglo-Saxon Protestant origin. It has been said that this phase of the nativist movement did much to end the open immigration that had for almost two preceding decades witnessed the arrival of some two million impoverished Irish Catholic immigrants. "Just a few short years later, Irish troops of the 69th Regiment emerged from the dense fog that blanketed Mayre's Heights in Fredericksburg, Virginia on the morning of December 13th, 1862, their ferocious war cry ringing out in their native Irish language...*Faugh a Ballagh... Faugh a Ballagh!*[27] In their ranks floated a green flag bearing, in the center, a golden harp. For several minutes, the Confederate defenders of the Heights poured a murderous fire into the crumbling, but courageous, ranks. So gallantly had the Confederate position been assaulted that members of a Georgia rifle company paused in their fire to cheer the bravery of the attackers before the murderous work commenced again.

At about the same time, a small group of dispirited men came together in New York City for what was to be the last recorded meeting of the Grand Council Committee of the Order of United Americans. In its heyday, the O.U.A. had spread through 16 states in the early 1850s, trumpeting its message of hatred against immigrants and Catholics. Now, its last pathetic remnant was unable to pay its bills or secure a quorum at meetings."[28]

Chapter 5

Stars And Stripes Have Been Dipped In The Blood Of Kings

The origins of the American Civil War were deep seeded and complex issues that stemmed from slavery and the rights of slave owners, different understandings of the doctrine of federalism, antagonistic sectional political differences, and economics. In the period from the founding of the United States, the political system attempted to deal with the issue of slavery, but not in a permanent sort of way. The Constitution of the United States called for holding the slavery question in abeyance until the year of 1808. While trafficking in the illegal slave trade slowly and eventually passed away, there was never any provision as to what was to happen with the slaves who were already the de facto property of many southern plantation owners, who greatly depended on slave labor to sustain the cash crop economy of the South. Neither the Missouri Compromise of 1820, nor the more complex, but equally indecisive, Compromise of 1850 ever held out the promise of the creation of a lasting solution; rather, both were mere stopgaps in a deadly and growing wave of bitterness and resentment between the North and South. By the

1850s, the desire of the slaveholders to control the national government was irreversibly in play.[1]

The United States, by 1860, had become thoroughly divided concerning the expansion of slavery and the rights of slaveholders. It was in this Presidential election year that the issues finally came to a dramatic head. As a result of the conflicting regional interests, the Democratic Party split into the Northern Democrats and Southern Democrats. A new Constitutional Union Party appeared, and lastly, the newly organized Republican Party, organized in Ripon, Wisconsin, fielding James C. Fremont as its first Presidential candidate in 1856, would now move to the fore in national politics. In this four-party contest, the Republican Party, dominant in many key northern states, would win enough electoral votes to put its candidate, Abraham Lincoln, into the White House. This would happen in spite of the fact that in many parts of the South, Lincoln did not even appear on the ballot for President. Within a few short months of Lincoln's election, seven southern states, with South Carolina in the lead, had seceded from the Union. In the wake of the firing on Fort Sumter on April 12th, 1861, four more southern states joined the ranks of the secessionists.[2]

I

Abraham Lincoln had served but a single term in the Congress (1847-49), and was a defeated candidate for the United States Senate, losing to Steven Douglas in 1858, but in spite of these reversals, he was to be elected the 16th President of the United States on November 6th, 1860. Lincoln, a virtual political unknown until his delivery of an address concerning the burning issue of slavery at Cooper Union in New York City, was a man who forged his Presidential ambitions by being cast as the "compromise" candidate acceptable to all, especially when prospects for the front runners made it unlikely any of them would be nominated. Chief contenders for the Republican nomination in 1860 were William H. Seward and Salmon P. Chase. While both possessed impressive anti-slavery credentials, it became more and more evident to the 10,000 delegates assembled in Chicago's newly built convention hall, the Wigwam, that neither man would be considered a moderate enough candidate to be acceptable to those persons looking to soften the rhetoric against certain aspects of the slavery issue, i.e., not interfering with it in the places where it already existed.

Lincoln's floor managers at the convention waged a brilliant campaign on behalf of their candidate, offering his as the best possible alternative candidacy to the men, who in the final analysis, simply could not be elected nationally.[3]

With Lincoln's election, the secession of the southern states from the Union, and the onset of four bloody years of civil war, Archbishop Hughes was to form a crucial and special relationship with the Lincoln Administration. Recognizing that Catholic countries such as France and even the Vatican harbored no great love for the United States, Lincoln had need as part of preserving the cause of the Union to be able and turn to a person, who by virtue of his esteem and experience, would be able to act as a voice for the American cause overseas...a person to whom the cause of preserving the Union would be given the dutiful and proper hearing so desperately needed by the Administration in Washington. Hughes's ardent pro-Americanism, coupled with fostering love of the land of the Irish Catholics in his spiritual care, was about to be put to the test in fire and steel on bloody battlefields with names like Antietam, Gettysburg, and Cold Harbor. On March 17th, 1860, while addressing the Hibernian Society of Charlestown, South Carolina, Hughes eloquently articulated the essence of the love he felt not only for nationality, but for the land of his origin: "Let the Irish people become educated, let them preserve the vigor of their national character and intellect, and they may bid defiance to the slang of pretended novel-writers. Their position already entitles them to the admiration of impartial and enlightened minds throughout the world. I trust, therefore, you will agree with me in sentiment, which I am about to propose, as being the most appropriate to this festive occasion in commemoration of Ireland's patron saint. I propose, gentlemen, as a sentiment: The Land of the Shamrock. No one born within its borders need be ashamed of his birthplace."[4]

In spite of the special talents a man of Hughes's caliber could offer in this type of diplomatic mission, Lincoln was to find no sympathetic understanding on the Archbishop's part with respect to the issue of slavery and its relation to the outbreak of hostilities between the North and South. To Hughes, the issue of greatest importance with respect to the war was not the injustice waged against the negro so much as the illegal and morally reprehensible act of secession. That Hughes vigorously opposed secession was no more clearly articulated than in his voluminous correspondence with many of the Catholic bishops of the South, one of whom was Patrick Nelson Lynch, Bishop of Charleston, South Carolina. Born in Ireland, Lynch was ordained to the priesthood in 1840 and had emerged as the premier Catholic spokesperson below the Mason-Dixon Line. Additionally, he had gained a reputation as an ardent supporter of the Southern cause, so much so that in 1864, Jefferson Davis was to ask him to plead the cause of the Confederacy to the Vatican – a mission which ultimately failed, leaving Lynch imprisoned in Rome until he was pardoned after the war. Hughes's objection to the southern position was not because of their slave society, but because he viewed secession as rebellion against the law of the land...the Constitution. Writing to Lynch on May 7th, 1861, Hughes responded to a previous letter from Lynch, who was attempting to justify the outbreak of hostilities and the dissolution of the Union:

"With regard to Catholics, North and South, I can have but little to say. I myself have never recommended any man to go to war, unless circumstances rendered it either expedient or necessary...Deprecating the assumed necessity for this war. I have not interfered by giving them advice to do so. It is the same with the South, I presume. But certainly there is a great difference in principle between the two sections of the country. The North have not been required to do anything new, to take an oath, support any new flag; they have kept on the even tenor of their way. The South, on the contrary, has taken upon itself to be the judge in its own cause, to be witness in its own cause, and to execute, if necessary, by force of arms, its own decision. In a constitutional country, this means either revolution or rebellion, since there are tribunals agreed upon by North and South, and supported by both for a period of more than seventy years."⁵

Similarly, in a letter to the Secretary of War, Simon Cameron, Hughes once again reiterated his extremely negative view of abolitionists and suggested that offering the manumission of slaves as a justification for going to war could only have the most negative impact on his people with respect to the Union cause:

> "There is being insinuated in this part of the country an idea to the effect that the purpose of this war is the abolition of slavery in the South. If that idea should prevail among a certain class [immigrant poor]," by implication, the Irish, "it would make recruiting slack indeed. The Catholics, as far as I know, whether of native or foreign birth, are willing to fight to the death for support of the Constitution, the Government, and the laws of the country, but if it should be understood that, with or without their knowing it, they are to fight for the abolition of slavery, then indeed, they will turn away in distrust from the discharge of what would otherwise be patriotic duty."⁶

The attack on Fort Sumter in Charleston Harbor by land artillery units under the command of General P. G. T. Beauregard in the early morning hours of April 12th, 1861, was the curtain riser of the bitter and bloody American Civil War. By the end of this national conflagration, almost four years to the day that the first shell arched high over Charleston Harbor before dropping down to its intended target, over 600,000 Americans would lose their lives. Rage and highly excited clamors for action shot across the North. In thousands of villages and towns, war meetings were organized against a backdrop of fifes, drums, and patriotically inflamed speeches.[7] The call to arms reached a fever pitch in places like New York City, where a massive war rally was held in Union Square on April 21st, 1861. Over 100,000 persons jammed the streets. Amidst the banners and streamers, dozens of New York notables such as John A. Dix, Daniel S. Dickinson, Fernando Wood, William F. Havemeyer, and D.D. and Hiram Ketchum made speeches and introduced resolutions. Although not able to be present on that day, the following letter was read to the mass of humanity assembled in and around the Square; the letter was from Archbishop John J. Hughes:

> "Unable to attend the meeting at Union Square, in consequence of indisposition, I beg to have my sentiments on the subject of your coming together in the following words: Ministers of religion and ministers of peace, according to the instruction of their Divine Master, are not ceased to hope and pray that peace and union may be preserved in this great and free country. At present, however, that question has been taken out of the hands of the peacemakers, and it is referred to the arbitrament of a sanguinary contest. I am not authorized to speak in the name of my fellow citizens. I think as far as I can judge, there is the right principle all among them, whom I know, it is now thirty years since, a foreigner by birth, I took the oath of allegiance to this country, under its title of the United

States of America. [Loud Cheers] As regards, conscience, patriotism, or judgment, I have no misgiving. Still desirous of peace, when the Providence of God shall have brought it. I may say that since the period of my naturalization, I have but one country.

"In reference to my duties as a citizen, no change has come over my mind since then. The Government of the United States was then, and it is now, symbolized by a national flag, popularly called "The Stars and Stripes." [Loud Applause] This has been my flag, and shall be to the end. [Cheers] I trust it is still destined to display in the gales that sweep every ocean, and amid the gentle breezes of many a distant shore, as I have seen it in foreign lands, its own peculiar waving lines of beauty, whether at home or abroad, for a thousand years, and afterwards as long as Heaven permits, without limit or duration."[8]

II

Irish Americans, as if embracing the opportunity to demonstrate their loyalty to the nation, rushed to join the clarion call of arms against the rebellious South. After decades of unrelenting bashing by the nativist Protestant elements, more than 140,000 men of Irish birth enlisted and fought for the Union, roughly a third from New York City. Of the Irish-fighting units that engaged in combat, none was to be more famous for its conspicuous gallantry than the New York Sixty-ninth Regiment (The Irish Brigade.) The unit was commanded by a soon-to-be military hero, Michael Corcoran, born in Donegal in 1827, and who immigrated to New York in 1849. Strong support of this effort came from the Irish Catholic hierarchy, most notably from Hughes. Soon after the attack on Fort Sumter, Hughes wrote confidentially to the Lincoln Administration that since the Sixty-ninth regiment consisted entirely of Irish Catholics, he took "a deep interest in the honor and bravery with which they shall conduct themselves calmly during the campaign."[9]

Although other regiments were organized, it was the Sixty-ninth regiment that ultimately came to symbolize Irish participation in the Civil War. On April 23rd, the regiment was given an enthusiastic send-off, with various Irish civic societies joining in the procession through the streets under "waving banners of the harp of Erin kissing the Stars and Stripes." Upon arrival in Washington D.C., it was once again received by a festive, cheering crowd of onlookers. In their debut engagement during the first Battle of Bull Run, in what was an otherwise calamitous defeat of Union forces, the Sixty-ninth held its position until ordered to withdraw, doing so in an orderly fashion. Their losses suffered on that day were heavy, including 39 who were killed. Colonel Corcoran was himself captured and held in a Confederate prison for a year.[10]

The death of so many was to have a profound effect on the Irish American community. Relief efforts were increased for those who went to the front, while the Friendly Sons of St. Patrick raised $1,500 dollars to equip and sustain the Sixty-ninth. Judge Charles P. Daly headed a committee to provide similar assistance for the Irish Seventy-fifth Regiment. The families left behind had little or no money, and the increased effort of relief committees mitigated to some extent the absence of that monetary support. By May of 1861, several thousand dollars had been raised, with the contributors vowing to continue supporting the troops for as long as they remained in the field.[11]

A mass meeting and festival at Jones Wood resulted in the largest assembly of contributors (sixty thousand) toward providing for relief of the widows and orphans of those who had given their lives in battle. At the expiration of the initial three month enlistment period of the first Union volunteer regiments, many of the Irish brigades saw high reenlistments, their members eager to return to the fight. *The Irish American* had urged the formation of one single, powerful Irish fighting force, no doubt calling to mind the stirring memories of the Irish brigades that had fought on the continent of Europe in service to monarchs and countries other than their own. Archbishop Hughes found the idea appealing as a means of protecting his Catholic faithful in a largely Protestant army; however, he quickly recognized that ethnic labeling of Irish, German, or other ethnic troops could prove troublesome before the enemy even came into sight. Because the Irish outfits were infused with the Catholic faith, in a predominantly, and at times, hostile military, Hughes was in favor of specifically using priests as chaplains in the Catholic regiments, as they were the protectors of the Faith, the holders of Catholic services, the hearers of confessions, and administrators of the last rites. Just as they had been agents of the social transformation of the Irish in their communities with respect to advocating religious devotion, sobriety, good, moral living, and regular attendance of mass and taking of the sacraments of the Church, so to would they now act as the agents of communication between the soldiers on the front and their families at home, proper use of their pay to take care of their

dependents, and even acting at times as bankers,
insuring that pay was transferred home, and also
taking charge of savings.[12]

President Lincoln, depended greatly on his liaison
with Hughes, was happy to receive what advice he
could with respect to "Catholic" issues, which for
Lincoln would have been matters reflective of limited
personal understanding, especially with respect to
appreciating motives for why reviled Irish Catholic
immigrants would participate in a war that was, on
the one hand, being waged in the name of the Union,
and on the other hand, preservation of a system that
excluded and castigated Irish Catholicism. Lincoln,
realizing the importance of this political block,
gingerly entreated Hughes with respect to advice on
the appointment of Catholic hospital chaplains:

> "I am sure you will pardon me, if in my
> ignorance, I do not address with technical
> correctness. I find no law authorizing the
> appointment of chaplains for our hospitals;
> and yet the services of chaplains are more
> needed, perhaps, in the hospitals, than with
> the healthy soldiers in the field. With this
> view, I have given a sort of quasi appointment
> (a copy of which I enclose) to each of three
> protestant ministers, who have accepted and
> entered upon their duties. If you perceive no
> objection, I will thank you to give me the
> names of one or two more suitable persons of
> the Catholic Church, to whom I may properly
> with propriety, tender the same service. Many
> thanks for your kind and judicious letters to
> Gov. Seward, and which he regularly allows
> me both the pleasure and profit of seeing."[13]

Hughes was now to take on the role of internationalist, not in the cause of battling nativism, which he had spent his entire priestly career doing, but in advancing the cause for preservation of the American Union. Lincoln, himself a master of placing competing personalities and adversaries into common cause and action with one another and himself, now turned to New York's Roman Catholic Archbishop. Originally reluctant to accede to Lincoln's request, Hughes's critical assignment was to provide a great service to his country in time of war. Before leaving, he was received by Lincoln at the White House and left fully realizing the critical mission with which he had been entrusted. With Thurlow Weed acting as his secretary, Hughes would travel to Ireland, Spain, Italy, and France...all of the Catholic countries of Europe, to enlist the support of and to promote the cause of the Union. Lincoln needed friends abroad, as well as friends at home, and Hughes, recognized not only internationally because of previous European trips, but as a prelate favored by the Pope.[14]

III

Through his great moral and financial support of the Pope and of the Vatican through the years, Hughes was the likely choice for such a mission. When viewed from the vantage point of European politics, the descent of the United States into civil war was viewed with a cynical satisfaction. England had greatly benefited from the southern cotton trade, and southern agents had boarded a British steamship, Trent, for the purpose of sailing to England with the intention of seeking recognition of the Confederacy. The commanding officer of the U.S.S. Jacinta,

Captain John Wilkes, had different ideas. His vessel stopped the British vessel, removing the agents James Mason and John Slidell immediately, placing both men under arrest. Wilkes was an instantaneous hero in the north and condemned abroad, especially in England, where his actions were viewed as an act of hostility against a sovereign nation. England prepared for war.[15] Among the first of his many stops, Hughes addressed a distinguished gathering of lay and churchmen at the time of the opening of Catholic University in Dublin, the first such Catholic University in Ireland:

> "Gentlemen, I will not say a word of America. I suppose I know as well as if I were born there, perhaps better, that there may be found there the weaknesses, passions, and prejudices that are more less the effect of mankind. I don't advise a single countryman of mine to go there if he can do well at home; still, I would say, in the presence of these venerable prelates and these devoted clergy who have consecrated their lives, I might say for the protection and salvation of their flocks...I would say to them, send us none who are drunkards, none who are bound up with secret societies in this, your land, whether Orangemen or Ribbonmen; give us good men, and now particularly is the time for them; men who will do honor to their country."[16]

Critics would later point to words like this as a hardly veiled attempt on the part of Hughes to recruit Irishmen into the ranks of the Union Army, when in fact, no proof of such activity could ever be shown to exist. So long as Irishmen sought out the shores of America to escape from the wretched economic and social conditions of their own land, Hughes was expressing a fervent hope that they would prove to be men of character and spirit, a character and spirit of the type to build better lives and strong nations. Again., in an address to the *Catholic Young Men's Society* during the same visit, he once again encouraged continued commitment to the elements needed by the Irish for success, whether in Ireland or America: "I thought I should meet with the *Catholic Young Men's Society*, to congratulate them upon the good which I have been told they are doing, sustaining each other in piety and in perseverance. I had no other purpose or object in view than to say to them a few words of encouragement. I intended to tell them how their countrymen in America, of the same professions, occupations, and condition in life, also labored in works of this kind; and I wish to encourage them in that way...To tell them that young Irishmen coming to America, if they are well inclined, if they are sober, but, above all, if they are unshackled by those...I would almost call them infernal bonds... secret societies; if they keep clear of these things, there is reasonable chance of success for them in America."[17]

Arrival of the political-clerical delegation in Paris posed different problems. U.S. Minister to Paris, William Dayton, proved uncooperative to Hughes, and was not enthusiastic with respect to helping someone whose status was that of an unofficial agent. Ultimately, he refused to arrange a meeting at court between Hughes, Emperor Napoleon, and Empress Eugenie. Fearing that the arrest of Mason and Slidell would have an equally negative effect on the French public as well, news of which was almost simultaneous with the Archbishop's arrival in Paris, it was decided that meeting with the Emperor should be arranged at once. The meeting eventually took place and was long, cordial, but inconclusive. Utmost in the mind of the Lincoln Administration was the damaging effect that recognition of the Confederacy by a European power could have on the outcome of the Civil War, which by 1862, had entered into its second bloody year. Hughes, in the course of his discussions with Napoleon and Eugenie, urged that in the event of war between the United States and England, France could mediate. Additionally, Hughes urged the French to break dependency on southern cotton by encouraging its culture and growth in Algeria. Another issue raised in the discussions pertained to the blockade of Cuba, an issue Hughes skillfully employed to enflame the passions and sensibilities of the Spanish Eugenie, by creating an image of the South seizing the whole Island of Cuba to expand its evil empire of slavery.[18]

The hot-blooded British were soon calmed in their war rhetoric, largely because of the backdoor intervention and quiet counsel of Victoria's consort, Prince Albert. The French, while making no commitments to Hughes, ultimately made Hughes to feel in his departure that there was no hard and fast sentiment for the French to recognize the Confederacy. Hughes, while having achieved more of a personal rather than diplomatic victory with Napoleon, felt less apprehensive, as Napoleon's address to the *Corps Legislatif* was one of much friendlier feelings toward the Americans than when he had first arrived.

In Rome, Hughes basked in and was the recipient of the Pope's favor. He again utilized this status as a means to promote the cause of Union, when meeting with pilgrims and high ecclesiastics from every corner of the Catholic world. Repeating the tactics he had used with Princess Eugenie, Hughes again assuredly advanced in his discussions with Spanish bishops how support of the Confederacy would result in their hold on Cuba being jeopardized.[19]

IV

The New York City of Hughes's early episcopacy had but a handful of scattered parishes spread out across New York State and northern New Jersey. By 1863, it was a vastly different diocese, a diocese where the population of Manhattan alone was about 800,000, about half of whom were foreign-born, and most being Irish. While the Irish Catholics of this first generation, many still not far removed from the blight of famine in their native land, slowly began to ascend the socio-economic ladder, there were still glaring inequities and sinister undercurrents among the Irish American community. While the valiant contribution of the Irish had not gone unnoticed by Native Americans in supporting the cause of the Union, there was still discrimination and prejudice. The Irish were still at the bottom of the ladder in the frustrating assimilation into American society. In spite of the advances being made, this frustration spilled over into unprecedented violence in the summer of 1863, a violence which seemingly undermined years of fighting to succeed and be remembered as one of the greatest acts of disloyalty by a people whose progress was predicated on the idea that they were, in fact, good and loyal Americans.

The draft had been instituted to continue a war effort that had largely been carried on by volunteer enlistments with fixed periods of service. At the end of the enlistment period, men could, and did, throw

away their arms because their period of service had
ended. This, coupled with the frightful casualties,
required Lincoln to devise a plan to keep a steady flow
of levees in readiness for fighting in the field. The
inequity of the draft was economic, as a person could
buy their way out of service for the sum of $300.00, a
sum that for the average workingman of the time,
would have represented an entire year's wages. It was
obvious where the brunt of the burden would fall in
New York, and everywhere, it was known as a "rich
man's war but a poor man's fight."[20]

Another factor contributing to the deeply suppressed anger of the Irish was with respect to free
blacks making their way to the north and competing
with the Irish for jobs, a competition being more and
more keenly and resentfully felt. The fast rise in the
cost of living as the result of the war was but another
powder bag being mixed into the cauldron of incendiary substances, requiring little to touch off the great
explosion. The drawing for the names of the con-
scripts began peacefully enough on Sunday, July
11th, 1863, even though the fires of discontentment
toward the draft were already being fanned. Democratic newspapers and ward politicians assured their
largely Irish foreign-born supporters that the Lincoln
Administration's tactics toward Democrats were
heavy-handed, oppressive, and even unconstitutional.
Throughout the day, as men flocked to their local
saloons to drink, Sunday being the only day of
relaxation and enjoyment for the average workingman, the undercurrents of anger sweeping one Irish
neighborhood after another became more pronounced
with the emptying of each barrel of beer. Self
appointed sidewalk orators did nothing to lessen the
rising tensions.

When Monday dawned, the omens of what was to come that day could already be felt in the steaming, foul, and oppressive humidity. At the draft offices located at Third Avenue and Forty-Sixth Street, a large crowd had assembled and commenced a fierce attack upon the buildings and its occupants just before noon. Many factory workers, as well as employees of the street railroads, joined the fracas. Fires were set, flames and smoke started to envelope the block, and when the first provost marshal's guard, along with a detachment of police, arrived, they were quickly overcome and scattered by the ever growing and drink-inflamed mob. "Every brute in the drove was pure Celtic, hod carrier, or loafer,"[21] recorded George Templeton Strong in his diary on that day.

The city exploded into violence as thousands of Catholic Irish immigrants burned, looted, and murdered at will, fighting the understaffed and overtaxed police force, and ultimately, troops rushed from the bloody battlefield of Gettysburg to aid the civil authority in putting down the uprising. The Irish showed a particular savagery with respect to blacks, as they burned a black orphanage to the ground, as well as hung black men from trees. The carnage continued for three days and was finally brought under control by the arrival from Pennsylvania of several battle-hardened regiments from the Army of the Potomac.[22]

After Hughes had labored for nearly 25 years in the assimilation and adaptation of his own people into American society; after the countless battles against nativist bigots to establish the right of his people to education, employment, and political enfranchisement, what could have gone so terribly wrong?

For the man, who in his sense of ultra-modernism, commenced the building of the new St. Patrick's Cathedral on Fifth Avenue, a testament not only to the Irish, but to the coming of age of Catholicism in America, he would not live to see the completion of this stunning architectural design. Old and infirm at the time of the draft riots, his response to the unruly and riotous mobs was both sullen and lethargic. Of all people, he, above anyone, could have called upon the Irish to cease and desist in the pillage and destruction engulfing the city. Governor Horatio Seymour appealed to Hughes to address his people from his Madison Avenue residence. Seymour wrote Hughes: "I do not wish to ask you anything inconsistent with your duties, but if you can, with propriety, aid the civil authorities at this crisis, I hope you will do so."[23] Hughes replied by circulating a letter with copies forwarded to the city's news publications asking all "Catholic" rioters to cease and desist from mob action and unchristian practices. He followed up with a notice that he would deliver an address on July 16th from the steps of his residence. Owing to medical considerations, the scheduled address of the 16th of July was in fact not delivered until the following day. Hughes, enfeebled with rheumatism, but nonetheless resolute in conviction, addressed about 5,000 persons from the steps of his home. He started the address by calling his listeners "my friends." He then continued by stating that some had gone astray. Those who had gone astray were Catholic, and so was he. They were Irish, and so was he. He further went on to say how the disturbances must stop for the sake not only of their Catholic religion, but for the sake of Ireland as well. A Union officer who heard the speech commented that "such an effort, if made four days earlier, would have prevented incalculable suffering and loss."[24] Hughes had given a good speech, and his followers dispersed peacefully and quietly, returning to their shacks, but in reality, the arrival of the army had made his speech academic. Hughes told the crowd:

> "Every man has a right to defend his home or his shanty at the risk of life. The cause, however, must be just. It must not be aggressive or offensive. Do you want my advice? Well, I have been hurt by the report that you were rioters. You cannot imagine that I could hear these things without being grievously pained. Is there not some way by which you can stop these proceedings and support the laws, none of which have been enacted against you as Irishmen or Catholics. You have suffered already. No government can save itself unless it protects its citizens. Military force will be let loose upon you. The innocent will be shot down and the guilty will be likely to escape."[25]

It will never be understood why Hughes took no more active part in quelling the disorders. It was true that he published an address to his people admonishing them to keep the peace, but this was prefaced by a long and bitter attack against Horace Greeley, owner and editor of the *New York Tribune*, and clearly demonstrated that he sympathized with the rioters, at least with respect to their condemnation of the draft. The suggestion that he would not have been safe while on the street was absurd, as priests mingled with the mob in many instances...not only without fear of their safety, but to good effect as well with the rioters. There was, however, one thing for certain about the mindset of the Archbishop, namely, had the mob threatened to burn down a Catholic Church, destroy Catholic property, or threaten to harm a Catholic clergyman, the mob would have been confronted with the most horrible wrath of the Church, and the lawless bands would have melted away in the face of the condemnations of their Archbishop.[26]

The draft riot of 1863 was not, as some conspiracy theorists advanced in the aftermath, a premeditated, calculated, Catholic insurrectionist plot. While it is beyond dispute that most of the rioters were Irish and Catholic, they were reacting collectively to the oppressive realities not only of New York in the 1860s, but of the country generally; namely, conditions were such that still excluded Irish Catholics from the broader society, while unfairly asking them to fight for preserving those benefits. It was also ironic that most of the New York police at that time were Irish-born men, and no police force ever demonstrated braver or more resolute action in the face of danger, or showed more courage and devotion to duty throughout the three days of rioting.

Five months later, the eminent prelate died in January of 1864. For twenty-six years, he had been as the lion, nurturing and protecting his growing Church, and raising his impoverished people to a status begrudging acceptance in American society. "Some of most prominent statesman of the time freely acknowledged that no man exercised more extensive influence on the public life of the country; and the impartial historian of the Church in the United States must admit that it was Archbishop Hughes, who in stormy and troubled times, laid the foundation of Catholic prosperity in the country. We are frequently reminded of the wonderful Providence of God, in scattering the faithful Irish Catholics in the famine years to plant the faith so securely in many corners of the world, and while we rejoice in the result, we cannot but deplore the oppression and misgovernment which robbed Ireland of the service of many preeminent statesman and leaders, among whom Archbishop Hughes will ever hold a conspicuous place."[27]. In the end, he was viewed as the leader of Catholics not only in New York, but in the entire country. His funeral was a major event in New York City, but not all found cause to mourn his passing. George Templeton Strong may have well reflected the feelings of Hughes's lifelong enemies:

> "Archbishop Hughes is dead. Pity he survived last June and committed the imbecility of his address to rioters last July. That speech blotted and spoiled a record which the Vatican must have held respectable, and against which Protestants had nothing to say, except of course, 'Babylon,' 'Scarlet Women' and 'anti-Christ.'"[28]

Chapter 6

"They May Do What They Like With The Diocese When I Am Under The Ground"

What was to be the legacy of John Joseph Hughes? He had assumed his episcopal mission in the New York diocese at a time when Catholicism was still a minority, passive, and insignificant religion. It had not yet cast itself into the social and political debates of the era because it was still lacking fearless and outspoken leadership. Hughes was to unapologetically take the raw material of his infant Church, namely, immigrants from his native Ireland, and build an urban-based ecclesiastical institution whose head would never again droop in shame before Native American bigots. Hughes would never have been content to head a gentile and invisible Church as his predecessors had done...a Church that would suffer silently for the greater good rather than fight for its place in America's quilt work. Hughes, in reacquainting his Irish flock with the power and majesty of the Catholic Faith, paved the way for the empowerment of his people politically. By stressing sobriety, discipline, devotion to their native and adopted land,

Hughes was training the Irish to take their place in an otherwise hostile society, a society that in a generation's time would be dominated by them. While Hughes believed that when possible, it was better for the typical immigrant of the famine to remain in the urban setting only long enough to gain bearings before moving out into the wide open country spaces where land and a life more akin to what he had known in Ireland awaited, he was also enough of a hard-headed realist to understand that the scattering of his people away from the concentrated urban center could result in their being cut off from the needed survival mechanisms such as active parish life, priests, and the confraternity of association with their own kind for aid and much needed moral support.

As allegiance to the Church would serve as a source of comfort and succor in spiritual matters, so too would allegiance to the Democratic Party and its urban political machine, reaping benefits in terms of material acquisition, and eventual advancement up the socio-economic ladder. Again, Hughes, the American nationalist, would be in the forefront of the cause of the Union, serving in a diplomatic capacity on behalf of Abraham Lincoln, a service backed by the blood of Irish-Americans demonstrating that same loyalty on the battlefield. The simple reality is that John J. Hughes was the first Roman Catholic churchman to achieve respect and notoriety as a Roman Catholic Churchman in his own right.

He had achieved standing in the eyes of both major political parties, and was consulted on a regular basis by both. Toward the end of the Civil War, the political deference extended to Hughes was carrying over to the other American Catholic prelates as well. It was a great testament to just how far the

Catholic Church in America had come when President
Andrew Johnson thought it advisable to attend the
closing session of the bishop's council in Baltimore in
1866. This transformation had not come about
through timidity and virtuous suffering in silence, but
by bold action, sometimes bordering on the violent.
For Hughes, leading his Church and his people over
the threshold of power, acceptance, and respect by
others, required dictatorial, single mindedness.
Though these accomplishments were needed for the
Catholic Church to cut its teeth in American society,
they could not mask what Hughes's critics would
have termed his "sins of omission" throughout his
long reign in New York.

The Irish were not the only Catholic immigrant
population in need of spiritual sustenance. There was
a sizable German Catholic population along with
French, Spanish, and African American Catholic
populations as well. To Hughes, it would seem as if
these communities within the larger community were
non-existent, and to a great extent, owing to circum-
stance, they were. The pre-famine Catholic population
of New York was compact and nonthreatening. The
German Catholic population of New York differed
greatly from their Irish counterparts. Firstly, the
German Catholics who came to America "went less to
build something new, as opposed to regain and
conserve something old."[1] Parish life was something
already known to the German Catholic community,
and this life was reinforced by use of the desired
medium of communication, the German language, a
medium which further strengthened the German
Catholic community in the creation of German
"National Parishes." While no strangers to poverty
within pockets of their own community, German
Catholics generally were not associated with the

acute economic distress of their Irish coreligionists. The indifferent attitude of Hughes toward the organization of German parishes reflected his policy of seldom interfering in their religious affairs. In his opinion, they exhibited a "narrow national feeling," and he found it "particularly difficult" to satisfy their demands; he was content to delegate this responsibility to his German Vicar General, John Raffeiner.[2] While Hughes did authorize and dedicate seven additional German churches and confirm German children, as an Irishman, he never bridged the gap separating him from the German Catholics of his diocese.[3]

Accordingly, to suggest that Hughes enjoyed episcopacy free of internal, as well as external, controversy would be falsehood. The well documented war of words waged in newspapers and correspondence on issues ranging from the proper place of parish trustees, Catholic school funding, Irish national organizations, and the proper place of religion within a democracy, is living testament to the pyretic state that existed during Hughes's tenure. Hughes was capable of his own obstinacy and stubbornness, at times authoritarian and impetuous. "He has," according to a Jesuit superior with whom he quarreled at Fordham, "an extraordinarily overbearing character; he has to dominate."[4] Provoking a reaction to Hughes's sometimes choleric disposition was much less complicated in the mind of a trustee of old St. Patrick's, who stated he would "horsewhip the bishop if he showed his face."[5]

In stark contrast to the bellicose style that characterized Hughes's dealings with the internal, as well as external, enemies of the Church were his cosmopolitan, conciliatory, and extremely popular diplomatic Vicar General of the Diocese and later

Archdiocese of New York, Father Felix Varela. Felix Varela y Morales was born in Havana, Cuba in 1788 at a time when Spain controlled not only the West Indies, but Louisiana, Florida, and much of what was then South America. His father was an officer in the Spanish regiment, and at an early age, young Felix demonstrated a marked inclination toward religious life. He was educated at the College and Seminary of San Jose and was ordained a priest in the year 1811. With the reinstitution of the Cortes[6] in Spain, Father Varela and two other select men were sent as representatives for the Island of Cuba to Madrid. An unrelenting opponent of slavery, Varela had presented a detailed proposal to accomplish the end of slavery in Cuba without doing harm to the rural white population.

Opposing his beliefs, the Holy Alliance, that compact of monarchs sworn to suppress social progress, along with the French armies aiding Ferdinand in his overthrow of the Cortes, Varela was driven into exile. Spending time first in New York and then Philadelphia, Varela continued his preaching and writing of themes connected to social justice and freedom for the oppressed. In 1825, at the invitation of Bishop John Connolly, Varela became attached to St. Peter's Church on Barclay Street in lower Manhattan. There was at that time only one other Catholic Church in New York – St. Patrick's on Mulberry Street. Varela's mission was now totally redirected to the fertile field of missionary outreach than so much a part of the embryonic Catholic Diocese of New York. When Jean Dubois was named Bishop in 1826, the new bishop experienced a difficult time in the handling of both the clergy and laity, a task that he relied and leaned most heavily on the Cuban refugee for help. As the population of St.

Peter's Church on Barclay Street started outstripping
the physical plant, Bishop Dubois instructed Fr.
Varela to start another church a little further north.
Using funds from his own inheritance and a small
group of Spanish friends, The Church of the
Transfiguration, "Father Varela's Church," was
consecrated in March of 1836. In its previous life, the
new church had been home to the Reformed Scotch
Presbyterian Church of Chambers Street.[7]

The ever growing Irish population had wanted
John Power to become bishop, and they greatly
resented the selection of the French-born Dubois. It
was here that Father Varela's touch did much to
soothe the accompanying tensions. Varela not only
learned and perfected his English, but studied Irish to
enable him to communicate in the native tongue of so
many Catholic Irish of the time. So impressed was
Dubois with the great humanitarian and pastoral
work of the Cuban priest, that he named Varela Vicar
General of the Diocese in 1837. "He was frequently
sent to the distant parts of the Diocese to settle
differences, to examine charges brought, and
represent the Right Reverend Bishop in most delicate
questions."[8] Varela would continue in the post of
Vicar General until his death in 1853. If Hughes
could be characterized as the iron fist, then Varela
was most certainly the velvet glove within which the
iron fist lay.

The coming of massive waves of Irish immigrants
who were destitute, unchurched, and unschooled,
however, required measures more drastic than the
cooling salve of diplomatic niceties. The task of
integrating such a group provided for Hughes a great
release of the pent-up energies within his spirit, a
spirit that at times presented itself as a mother in
unqualified defense of her children. Not surprisingly,

as in any closely knit family, elements within the otherwise adoring Irish community were to have passionate disagreements with their surrogate parent. No issue greatly illustrated this more true than the emergence of a virulent Irish nationalism resurrected in the wake of the revolutions that spread across Europe in 1848. The New York Irish community came to reflect the fractious and often strident divisions that existed within the nationalist movement in Ireland. Every group had its supporters, advocates, and publications, with support for one or another, causing rifts within churches, benevolent societies, and the press.

I

Because of its strategic location as a port of entry and the rapidly growing Irish community, New York became headquarters for the Repealers, The Young Ireland Movement, Fenians, and countless other organizations involved in the cause of throwing off hated English rule in Ireland. Irish political refugees John Devoy, John O'Mahony, John Mitchel, and Jeremiah O'Donovan Rossa came to New York and used the New York Irish community as a springboard for political action. Irish nationalism and independence consequently became interwoven into the local politics of New York.[9] While there is no doubt that Hughes greatly hated British rule in his native land, he nonetheless admonished and preached to his people a different path, a path that stressed assimilation and loyalty to their newly adopted land. He preached against participation in secret societies, a hallmark of Irish revolutionary activity, and further admonished his flock to not be taken up by revolutionary movements that had been both short-lived and prone to failure throughout Irish history. To Hughes, many of the Young Irelanders were tainted with irreligion: French radicalism had corrupted their minds. One of the leaders that Hughes was to take to task was the fiery orator Thomas D'Arcy McGee of the New York Irish publication *Nation.* McGee had made the charge that the priests and bishops of Ireland had been the primary cause for failure of the rebellion. Hughes, responding to this charge in the *Freeman's Journal*, replied:

> "The clergy would have been faithless to the obligations of religion and humanity, if they had not interposed, seeing as they must have seen the certain and inevitable consequence of a movement so nobly conceived, but so miserably conducted."[10]

Hughes further stated how the followers of McGee's school of thinking was that of an "Irish tribe whose hearts have apostatized from the honored creed of their country, but whose lips have not yet mustered the bad courage to disavow the faith of their forefathers."[11]

For Hughes, the Church was the key, and Hughes did everything in his power to focus that Church on the needs of the Irish masses in the spiritual realm, as well as temporal needs through schools, hospitals, parishes, and sound Catholic religious practice and character formation. Due to the tightly knitted urban setting, it was guaranteed that the Irish would eventually flex their muscle to demand their proper recognition and place.

As a strong defender of the Union, he zealously opposed the Southern rebellion. Hughes never wavered in these views, even after Lincoln's Emancipation Proclamation. As to the charges of his critics that he supported slavery, while he was not in favor of the manumission of slaves, at least not in an immediate fashion, he most definitely advocated dignified treatment in the face of the mostly cruel and inhuman conditions in which slaves lived. As his Irish community competed with free blacks for the lowest positions on the socio-economic ladder, Hughes would not have likely been swayed by arguments endorsing improved conditions of blacks over his own struggling and desperately impoverished people. This would have been true regardless of who the Irish were forced to compete against for society's crumbs. In this respect, he was more intellectually honest than the abolitionists, who he considered the most blatant of hypocrites. While agitating for the manumission of slaves, there were few abolitionists who would maintain that blacks, upon being freed in American society, should assume a place of equality with the white man. To Hughes, the abolitionist view of slavery of the black man as "unchristian" was totally inconsistent with respect to Irish Catholic immigrants. Many abolitionists harbored nativist antipathy toward the Irish, and to Hughes, their brand of Christianity with respect to Irish struggling in American society was hardly Christ like.

As to why Hughes, after his years of successful labor, his dramatic increasing of the size of the New York Archdiocese, and his reformation of a religiously and socially lost race of people, never achieved the crowning glory of a Red Hat or the making of New York as a Cardinalate See while no doubt, subject to much conjecture, may indeed be attributable to numerous concrete factors.. Hughes, throughout his tenure in New York, certainly enjoyed general approval from the Vatican and the Pope himself. He was always a vigorous defender of the Pope as head not only of the Universal Church, but as head of a twenty-province country populated by some three million persons across a broad swath of land extending through north central Italy. Generally considered the worst run and most inefficient government in Europe, the Papal States rocked and broiled for decades from the brutality of troops under unrestrained Cardinals, dishonesty, self-seeking favoritism, and revulsion against "liberal" ideas of any kind. Hughes, who had, at times, a reputation for letting his emotions outstrip his common sense, had proposed raising a volunteer American army to be at the Vatican's disposal for fighting purposes similar to what his pole star, Cardinal Cullen, had done in Ireland. Fortunately, his proposals, which had been contained in personal correspondence to Rome, never found their way into American newspapers.[12]

Perhaps it was for the combative approach he had assumed and thrived on through the long years of his rein in relation to enemies, both within and without the Church, his inconsistent financial administration, or the seemingly flagrant non-involvement with any other than the Irish community of his diocese. Perhaps it was because European heads of state, the Vatican included, looked with a hardly veiled contemptuous grin at America as its high and mighty liberal experiment in democracy dissolved into civil war, rebuffing even a request from President Lincoln to consider Hughes for being made a Cardinal. Support of this contention may be found in a letter written by Hughes to his friend, Secretary of State William Seward, and published in *The New York Times* on November 1st, 1862. In this letter written after Hughes's return from an extensive trip on behalf

of Abraham Lincoln to bolster the cause of the Union
with Catholic European heads of state, Hughes wrote
sadly of the negative view of America existing within
these quarters:

> "On the other hand, I may say that no day –
> no hour even – was spent in Europe in which
> I did not, according to opportunity, labor for
> peace between Europe and America. So far,
> that peace has not been disturbed. But let
> America be prepared. There is no love for the
> United States on the other side of the water.
> Generally speaking, on the other side of the
> Atlantic, the United States are ignored, if not
> despised; treated in conversation in the same
> contemptuous language as we might employ
> toward the inhabitants of the Sandwich
> Islands, or Washington Territory, or Van-
> couver's Island, or the settlement of the Red
> River or of the Hudson Bay's Territory. This
> may be considered very unpolished, almost
> unchristian language proceeding from the pen
> of a Catholic Archbishop. But, my dear
> Governor, it is unquestionably true, and I am
> sorry to say that it is so. If you, in
> Washington, are not able to defend yourselves
> in case of need, I do not see where or from
> what source you can expect friendship or
> protection."[13]

America was mission territory, and would be
considered so until 1908. Americans would, for quite
some time, come to be considered spiritually imma-
ture and unsophisticated. Even though Hughes's
successor, John McCloskey, would be the first
American so honored, his elevation to Cardinal would

reflect a broader reality with respect not only to the New York Archdiocese, but the American Catholic Church generally as pertains to filling the highest echelons of leadership.

II

The Roman Catholic population of the United State tripled in the years between 1860 and the end of the century. Numbering some 7,000,000 persons, the Catholic Church had emerged as the largest religious denomination in the country, with Irish representation holding the majority. The seminal work of Hughes in building up the New York Diocese, crown jewel of the American Catholic Church, had been prodigious. In the years between 1842 and 1863, an unprecedented number of Catholic churches were established in New York, testament to the bold and aggressive program of building a community of Faith.[14] Greatly aided by improvements in transportation and the dramatic increase in population, Hughes oversaw the establishment of Roman Catholicism as a majority religion. Nothing approximating the growth of the Hughes tenure would occur in New York until the reign of Francis Cardinal Spellman (1939-1967), whose aggressive posturing with respect to the Catholic Church and aggressive program of church and parish building would earn him the appellation, "American Pope."[15]

CHURCHES ESTABLISHED IN THE NEW YORK
DIOCESE DURING THE HUGHES EPISCOPACY

Church	Year of Foundation	Location
St. Andrew	1842	Duane St.
Nativity	1842	2nd Ave. & 2nd St.
St. Raymond	1842	Bronx, N.Y.
Assumption of the BVM	1842	Brooklyn Heights
St. Patrick	1843	Verplanck
St. Patrick	1843	Fort Greene, Bklyn.
Sts. Peter and Paul	1844	Williamsburg, Bklyn.
Holy Redeemer (German)	1844	E. 3rd St.
St. Francis (German)	1844	W. 31st St.
St. Columbia	1845	W. 25th St.
St. Mary	1845	Wappingers Falls
St. Joseph	1845	Croton Falls
St. Alphonsus (German)	1847	Thompson St.
St. Francis Xavier	1847	W. 16th St.
St. Stephen	1848	E. 28th St.
St. Brigid	1848	Ave. B & 8th St.
St. Peter	1848	Haverstraw
Our Lady of Fatima	1848	Scarsdale
Our Lady of Mercy	1848	Port Chester
Immaculate Conception	1848	Yonkers

Church	Year of Foundation	Location
St. Augustine	1849	Bronx, N.Y, 167th, St. (Fulton & Franklin Aves.)
St. Charles Borromeo	1849	Brooklyn Heights
St. John The Evangelist	1849	Park Slope, Bklyn.
St. Thomas	1850	89th St.
St. Ignatius Loyola	1851	980 Park Avenue
Immaculate Conception	1851	Port Jervis
St. Mary	1852	Bay Street, Sl
Holy Cross	1852	W. 42nd St.
St. Martin de Porres	1852	Poughkeepsie
St. John	1852	Piermont
St. Ann	1852	E. 8th St.
Immaculate Conception	1853	150th St. & Melrose Ave., Bx., N.Y.
St. Augustine	1853	Eagle Park
St. Theresa of Avila	1853	Sleepy Hollow
Annunciation	1853	W. 131st St.
Blessed Sacrament	1853	New Rochelle
St. Mary	1854	Obernburg
Immaculate Conception	1855	E. 14th St.
Our Lady of Mercy	1855	Westchester-later (Fordham Rd. and Marion Ave., Bx,. N.Y.)

Church	Year of Foundation	Location
Incarnation	1855	14th St. & 1st Ave.
St. Michael	1857	W. 32nd St.
Assumption (German)	1858	W. 50th St.
St. Boniface (German)	1858	20th Ave. & 47th
St. Paul	1858	W. 60th St.
New St. Patrick's Cathedral	1858	51st St. & 5th Ave.
Church of the Assumption	1859	Peekskill
St. Gabriel	1859	E. 37th St.
St. Joseph (German)	1860	W. 125th St
St. John	1860	W. Hurley
St. Teresa	1862	Rutgers St.
St. Joseph	1862	Rhinecliff
Sacred Heart	1862	Dobbs Ferry

In the 1840s and 50s, the anti-Irish Catholic reaction had been an urban concentrated affair; by the end of the 19th century, the focal point of nativist vitriol had shifted to remote places like Nebraska and Michigan. Even the cross burnings of the Ku Klux Clan in the early years of the 20th century were generally carried out in areas where Catholics were as remote in numbers as cathedrals. Nonetheless, the strident Protestant tone of America before the Civil War, its aggressive nativist crusade against Roman Catholicism, and by association, the Irish, forced the Catholic Church to remove itself from any effort to accommodate urban institutions and sought to establish a totally separatist structure of schools, social institutions, hospitals, orphanages, financial institutions, and benevolent associations. In New York, the city government, rooted in a totally Protestant culture, could not, and would not, meet the needs of an expanding Irish Catholic community, and so the Irish, aided and encouraged by Bishop Hughes, did it themselves. Regardless of the failure of John Hughes to be made a member of the College of Cardinals, he did succeed greatly in making the Catholic Church in New York a bulwark that politicians learned they could not carelessly hit up against and that Protestants could no longer ignore.[16]

His critics would greatly castigate Hughes for forcing his people into a narrow and limited path, a path they claimed that would work more to limiting their progress than advancing it. In the guarding and protection of his flock against the unjust attacks and prejudices of the time, Hughes, while stressing assimilation and blending on the one hand, was simultaneously removing his Church and "Catholic" institutions from an unfriendly society. For models of growth and development, the Catholic Church in New York had no models to follow except for the one that had existed in Ireland, and this was a model of extremely intense conservatism. The Church's social apostolate followed the same trend as did the pattern of politics when the Irish took control of the machinery of government. As Hughes saw it, the purpose of his Church was the preservation of the old order, an order that in the past had been robbed from his people by an alien English oppressor. While undoubtedly this was to prove one of its greatest strengths, as long as its outreach was immigrant focused, the Catholic Church's conservatism was to remain firmly intact. Even as the Irish immigrant community continued to evolve and become more American, the time of "foundation" had chartered the course the Church was to follow in the future. The success of Hughes's urban Church in places like New York was to be the measurement of the Church's achievement in the rest of the country. Hughes's legacy, however, of building insular walls around the Church was to form the basis of bitter contention amongst the Catholic hierarchy during the last quarter of the 19th century.[17]

Within 15 years of Hughes's death, the Catholic Church in the United States had grown so numerous and powerful politically that its view with respect to its place in the United States was greatly in need of redefining. The fundamental question was whether the Church should once again seek to be more assimilated with American institutions or whether it should continue down the solo, separatist path that had been laid down by Hughes? The terms of this controversy were to be bitterly fought out between the hierarchy's "assimilationists" or "Americanists" as they would come to be known, and the conservatives. Not for another century, in the bitter disputes that followed the proceedings of the Second Vatican Council, would the level of vitriol between American Roman Catholic Churchmen ever be greater. The momentous issues that would seed the savage battleground would be the Church's stance on issues such as labor unions, ethnic assimilation, social reform, and the parochial school system itself.[18]

Beyond these issues in the emerging American Catholic Church, a more subtle reality governed the promotion of men to the highest offices, and this reality, probably more than any other, was the main inhibitor to Hughes's further promotion in the hierarchy. While the Irish from Hughes's time provided a disproportionately high number of priests to labor in the trenches, the path to real power lay in the bureaucratic, rather than pastoral, aspects of the clerical life. A Roman education and Roman patronage were needed for success in the corridors of Vatican power.

In the quarter century following Hughes's death, The Vatican finally came to grips with the realization of the potential of the American Catholic Church, in terms of membership, influence, and finance. The fulfillment of Cardinal Cullen's ambitious dream of Catholic suzerainty in the United States, however, unquestionably rested firmly on the pilings sunk into the ground by the unyielding tenacity of Hughes. To Hughes had fallen the formidable task of securing the beachhead, and getting the troops ashore. Once secured, his personality and talents best served surviving the long artillery siege that preceded the ability of his troops to make their inroads. To others, and not Hughes, would come the glorious breakout and move to capture the ultimate objective – accommodation with and acceptance of Catholicism as the de facto preeminent religious group in the United States. The great strength of Hughes in fighting the good fight to build something was simultaneously to be the source of his undoing; however, he relished the part and played it willingly and well.

III

As well as spiritual foundation, Hughes was the creator and driving force behind the means of "material" foundation for his Irish immigrant community as well, and the result was no less spectacular with the creation of the means for his people to establish financial thrift, savings, and the ability to harness the monetary resources needed for helping those left behind in Ireland. In this regard, the foundation of the Emigrant Savings Bank, created under the auspices of Hughes in conjunction with Irish bankers and merchants, most notably Hughes's countryman, Eugene Kelly, was a milestone in the life of the post famine Irish immigrant community in New York. Established at 51 Chambers Street, it opened its doors for business on the morning of September 30th, 1852. The first deposit of funds was made by Bridget White in the amount of one hundred dollars, a sum roughly equivalent to twenty-five hundred dollars in today's currency. Proud of her ability to make this deposit, the occasion for White may have passed without any further noteworthiness, except that when she was leaving the bank, she encountered the Right Reverend Archbishop John J. Hughes on his way in to make a deposit himself.[19]

The Emigrant Bank was no ordinary financial institution, for it was the brainchild of Hughes and some of his Irish mercantile and banking friends, founded for the purpose of providing the thousands of Irish immigrants flooding into New York City a place to save money and forward remittances to help people back in Ireland. An outgrowth of the Irish Emigrant Society, which had been founded in 1840 for the purpose of helping newly arrived Irish find employ-ment and send money back home, its creation represented a first in that as a banking institution, it catered to the needs of the Irish. Whereas medical, charitable, benevolent, and educational organizations had been most representative of the organized outreach to the needy Irish immigrant community, The Emigrant Bank represented a crucial step in the building of financial confidence and independence. The principle center for the Irish to practice savings and thrift, the bank grew rapidly. By 1850, the

Emigrant had been chartered by the New York State Legislature. By 1856, it could boast over 11,000 accounts with $1,300,000 dollars in deposits.[20]

One of the other prominent characteristics of the bank is that it was the depository for many catholic priests, as well as the bank to hold parish funds in trust. That so many clergy opened and maintained accounts, not the least being the Archbishop himself, did much to cement in the minds of the Irish Catholic community that the Emigrant Savings Bank was "their" bank. Aside from the obvious benefits of bolstering a sense of financial responsibility in the new country, as well as providing some semblance of financial care for those left behind in the old, Hughes and many of his clergy set the greatest and most powerful example for their flock by leading in the effort to engage in some kind of disciplined savings.[21]

Toward the end of what had been a long, fruitful, and thorny governance of the New York Church, it is so humanly inconceivable that the thought of the final prize of the Cardinal's red zucchetto alluding Hughes should never have crossed his mind. Growing feeble in his advancing age, his long labor for the Church and his beloved Irish community not surprisingly had oftentimes left him in a state of oppressive fatigue. He entertained the idea of resigning his office so that he could pursue his other life joys of reading and study, pursuits not often possible during his intensively active ministry.[22] During the Civil War, for example, he would often study the geography and strategic points of the country like a military man, becoming intensely interested in the study of and movement of troops from one location to another. He expressed to Rome his wish to retire, but the prefect of the Propaganda, Cardinal Barnabo would not entertain such a request.

Hughes asked for a coadjutor, that is, another bishop to assist in the administration of diocesan affairs, who in theory would become Hughes's successor. Such a request could be clearly interpreted as a sign that he was breaking down. It was only a few years before that Hughes had asserted to a friend, "They may do what they like with the diocese when I am under the ground, but so long as I live, there shall be no coadjutor bishop of New York."[23] For the man who had built a diocese out of a patchwork of scattered and financially failing churches, battled the ugly face of nativism, raised up an immigrant Irish community to assume their place in America through the establishment of schools, political, social, and benevolent societies, was instrumental in the creation of the first financial institution for the nascent Irish Catholic community in New York, defender of the Union, councilor to Presidents and unofficial foreign minister of the United States to the courts of Europe, his demise was not in conformity with the strident and acrimonious road he had so often travelled.

In the end, the old lion quietly retired more and more from the public gaze, himself declining to enter any longer into the arena. Bishop, later Cardinal John McCloskey, was to give us, in a few sentences from his funeral oration of John Hughes, the key elements of the success of all his undertakings: "There was one trait that distinguished the Archbishop most particularly. It was his singular force and clearness and vigor of intellect, his strength of will, and firmness of resolution. He was a stranger to fear. His heart was full of undaunted courage. In the presence of dangers and difficulties, his energies only seemed roused to greater strength and higher exertion. He never quailed in the presence of any difficulty or trial. Not that he trusted wholly and solely on himself. He trusted in his cause and he trusted in God, to whose service he had pledged himself and devoted his entire being."[24]

Perhaps there is no more fitting tribute of the love and devotion John Hughes had for his people and adopted land than expressed in the following poem, one of many he composed throughout the course of his active, fruitful, and controversial life:

Jubilee of American Freedom

Great Lord of Creation, we owe it to thee,
That our country is kingless, our people are free!
Oh, grant a like boon to that ill fated Isle,
Where the ruled are as brave as their rulers are vile;
Where genius illumines, and minds are sincere;
Where hearts beat in bosoms that never felt fear;
Yes, children of freemen, your fathers could tell,
How the Irishman fought till he conquered or fell;
How the hero stood still when the heartless were flying
How Arnold betrayed while Montgomery was dying!
Poor Erin, thy sons shall have fame in our story;
Their sickles were mixed in our harvest of glory.
Columbia invites thee to rise and be free,
Till she call thee her sister, thou gem of the sea,
But, hark! Oh that song swelling higher and higher!
'Tis the voice Columbia, attuned to the lyre;
'Tis her thanksgiving anthem, and millions combine
In the chorus of love around Liberty's shrine.

Peace to the patriot, setting in glory
His eye hath grown dim, and his locks have grown
    hoary.
He balanced no scepter, he cushioned no throne;
He was wise for his country, his country alone.

Peace to the ashes of heroes that sleep.
In the battle-field grave, or the cells of the deep.
Their deeds be the theme of both story and art,
But their names are inscribed in the book of my
    heart.[25]

Though a man of humanly shortcomings, Hughes's life was one of stewardship over those who were weak, sick, hungry, and reviled. His life was a discordant symphony in the fight against hatred and xenophobia. Suspecting that he could have equaled the "Native American" or old "Know-Nothing Party" member in singing with gusto about the land he loved, he strove to establish the right of a nation within a nation to achieve a place at the table. For those whose betterment, opportunity, and dignity he fought to uphold and preserve, namely, the Catholic Irish immigrants of the great Irish diaspora, he earned a well deserved throne in the pantheon of American heroes.

THE BISHOPS, ARCHBISHOPS AND CARDINAL-ARCHBISHOPS OF THE ROMAN CATHOLIC DIOCESE OF NEW YORK

Bishops

R. Luke Concanen	1808-1810
John Connolly	1814-1825
John Dubois	1826-1842
John Joseph Hughes	1842-1850

Archbishops / Cardinal Archbishops

John Joseph Hughes	1850-1864*
John Cardinal McCloskey	1864-1885**
Michael Augustus Corrigan	1885-1902
John Murphy Cardinal Farley	1902-1918
Patrick Joseph Cardinal Hayes	1919-1938
Francis Cardinal Spellman	1939-1967
Terrence John Cardinal Cooke	1968-1983
John Joseph Cardinal O'Connor	1983-2000
Edward Michael Cardinal Egan	2000-2009
Timothy Michael Cardinal Dolan	2009-Present

* John Joseph Hughes was the fourth bishop of the New York Diocese, and became the first Archbishop when New York was raised to an Archdiocesan See in 1850.

** Archbishop John McCloskey was the first American to be elevated to the College of Cardinals, and the first Cardinal-Archbishop of the New York Archdiocese.

Chapter Notes

Foreword

1. Redemptioner- a person whose passage was paid to the American Colonies in exchange for a contract to work for a period of time necessary to repay the advanced funds.

2. John Higham, *Strangers in the Land* (New York: Atheneum, 1969), 6-7.

3. Daniel Walker Howe, *What Hath God Wrought: The Transformation of America, 1815-1848,* (New York: Oxford University Press), 320-321.

4. Thomas J. Shelley, Archbishop John Hughes and the Church in New York, Catholic New York, July, 2000. http://cny.org/archive/ft/070600.htm.

5. Land of Eoghan - English translation for the Irish, *Tir Eoghan,* which in its Anglicized form is "Tyrone," the Irish County in the Province of Ulster that was the birthplace of Bishop Hughes.

Chapter 1

"Do Not Forget The Charity That Is Due To Persons"

1. Quoted in Graham Hodges, "*Desirable Companions and Lovers:*" *Irish and African Americans in the Sixth Ward, 1830-1870,* Ronald H. Bayor and Timothy J. Meagher, *The New York Irish,* ed. (John Hopkins Press, 1996), 117.

2. Marcus L. Hansen, *The Atlantic Migration, 1607-1860* (Cambridge: Cambridge University Press, 1940), 41.

3. Robinson, Philip, *The Plantation of Ulster* (St. Martin's Press, 1984), pp.52-55.

4. E.R.R. Green, "*The Great Famine, 1845-1850:*" *The Course of Irish History,* ed., T.W. Moody and F.X. Martin (Cork, Ireland: Mercier Press, 1967), 274.

5. Partible Inheritance - the practice of dividing land among all sons.

6. Helen Litton, *The Irish Famine: An Illustrated History* (Dublin: Wolfhound Press, 1994), 15.

7. Ibid, 15.

8. E.R.R. Green, "*The Great Famine, 1845-50:*" *The Course of Irish History,* ed. T.W. Moody and F.X. Martin (Cork, Ireland: Mercier Press, 1967), 274.

9. John Higham, *Strangers In The Land* (New York: Atheneum, 1963), 6.

10. Robert J. Rayback, *Millard Fillmore* (Buffalo Historical Society, 1959), 386-414.

11. James G. Leyburn, *The Scotch-Irish: A Social History* (University of North Carolina Press, 1962), 327-334.

12. Thomas J. Shelley, "Archbishop John Hughes and the Church in New York," Catholic New York, July, 2000, http://cny.org/archive/ft/ft070600.htm.

13. Ibid, Quoted in Thomas J. Shelley.

14. William J. Stern, "How Dagger John Saved New York's Irish," City Journal, Spring, 1997, http://www.city-iournal.org/html/7 2a2.html.

15. Lawrence Kehoe, ed., *Complete Works of the Most Rev. John Hughes, D.D., Archbishop of New York, Comprising His Sermons, Letters, Lectures, Speeches, Etc., Vol.2,* (New York: Lawrence Kehoe, 7 Beekman Street, 1866), 268.

16. Jay P. Dolan, *The Immigrant Church, New York's German and Irish Catholics 1815-1865* (John Hopkins University Press, 1977), 2-3.

17. Ibid, 46.

18. Oscar Handlin, *The Uprooted* (Grosset & Dunlop, 1951), 125.

19. Jay P. Dolan, *The Immigrant Church, New York's German and Irish Catholics, 1815-1865*, p. 54

20. *The New York Times*, August 16th, 1858.

21. Charles R. Morris, *American Catholic, The Saints and Sinners Who Built America's Most Powerful Church* (Times Books, 1997), 9.

22. *The New York Times*, May 26th, 1879.

23. Charles R. Morris, *The Saints and Sinners Who Built America's Most Powerful Church*, 9.

24. Ibid, 10.

25. Ibid, 10-11.

26. Ibid, 14.

Chapter 2

Holding On To What Little Remains

1. Handlin, *The Uprooted*, 117.

2. Rev. Henry A. Bran D.D., *John Hughes, First Archbishop of New York* (Dodd, Mead and Company, 1892), 15.

3. Ribbonmen - network of secret Catholic organizations dedicated to physical confrontation with Protestants.

4. Orangemen - network of Protestant organizations
    devoted to the humiliation, and physical con-
    frontation with Roman Catholics.

5. G.A. Hayes-McCoy, "The Tudor Conquest, 1534-
    1603:" *The Course of Irish History*, ed. T.W.
    Moody and F.X. Martin, 183.

6. Ibid, 217.

7. Ibid, 218.

8. Ibid, 218.

9. Ibid, 219., Quoted in G.A. Hayes-McCoy.

10. Nathan Glazer and Daniel P. Moynihan, *Beyond
    the Melting Pot: The Negroes, Puerto Ricans, Jews,
    Italians and Irish of New York City*, (Cambridge,
    Mass.: MIT Press, 1970), 232.

11. Ibid, 232.

12. J.H. Whyte, "The Age of Daniel O'Connell, 1800-
    1847:" *The Course of Irish History*, ed. T.W.
    Moody and F.X. Martin, 249.

13. Ibid, 248.

14. Ibid, 250.

15. Ibid, 250., Quoted in J.H. Whyte.

16. Ibid, 252.

17. Ibid, 254.

18. Ibid, 256.

19. Ibid, 258., Quoted in J.H. Whyte.

20. Ibid, 261.

21. Virginia Crossman, *Politics, Law and Order in 19th Century Ireland*, (Dublin: Gill and Macmillan, Ltd., 1996), Paragraph 1 of Introduction.

22. Ibid.

Chapter 3

"This Is An English Colony, With Anglo-Saxon Contempt For Everything Irish"

1. Helen Litton, *The Irish Famine*, 108.

2. David Fitzpatrick, "Flight From Famine:" *The Great Irish Famine*, ed. Cathal Poirteir (Dublin: Mercier Press, 1995), 179.

3. Ibid, 181.

4. Leo Hershkowitz, "The Irish and the Emerging City, Settlement to 1844," Ronald H. Baylor and Timothy Meagher, *The New York Irish*, ed., 20.

5. Extract from "Parochial Records," Diocese of Clogher, by Rev. J.E. McKenna, P.P., Printed in the "Fermanagh Herald" Office, Enniskillen, 1920.

6. Reverend Henry A. Bran, *Most Reverend John
    Hughes: First Archbishop of New York*, (New York:
    Dodd, Mead and company, 1892), 18-19.

7. Reverend Henry A. Bran, *Most Reverend John
    Hughes: First Archbishop of New York*, 30.

8. Ibid, 34.

9. Ibid, 34.

10. Ibid, 34., Quoted in Reverend Henry A. Bran.

11. Ibid, 36., Quoted in Reverend Henry A. Bran.

12. "Whore of Babylon" - In the traditional Protestant
    lexicon of anti-Catholic bigotry, the "Whore of
    Babylon" was always understood to be the Pope
    and Catholic Church. The expression comes from
    the Book of Revelation, the last Book of the New
    Testament.

13. Quoted in Richard Shaw, *Dagger John: The Unquiet
    Life and Times of Archbishop John Hughes of New
    York* (New York: Paulist Press, 1977), 93.

14. Charles R. Morris, *The Saints and Sinners Who
    Built America's Most Powerful Church*, 54.

15. Ibid, 55-59., Quoted in Charles Morris.

16. The Reverend Henry A. Bran, *Most Reverend
    John Hughes*, 50-53.

17. Lawrence Kehoe, ed., *The Complete Works of the
    Most Reverend John Hughes, D.D., Archbishop of*

New York, Volume 1, (New York: Lawrence Kehoe, 7 Beekman Street, 1866), 8.

18. William J, Stern, "How Dagger John Saved New York's Irish," City Journal, Spring, 1997, http://www.city-iournal.org/html/ 72a2.html.

19. Publius Cornelius Tacitus - Roman historian who authored among his many works *The History of Imperial Rome*

20. John Higham, *Strangers In The Land,* 9-10.

21. Ibid, 10.

22. Gaius Julius Caesar, *Caesar's War Commentaries, De Bello Gallico and De Bello Civili,* (Kessinger Publishing, 2000), 103.

23. Maire and Conor Cruise O'Brien, *A Concise History of Ireland,* (New York: Beekman House, 1972), 15.

24. Daniel Walker Howe, *What Hath God Wrought: The Transformation of America, 1815-1848,* (New York: Oxford University Press), 285-288.

25. Ibid, 320.

26. Thomas J. Shelley, "Archbishop John Hughes and the Church in New York."

27. Lawrence Kehoe, ed., *The Complete Works of the Most Reverend John Hughes, D.D., Archbishop of New York, Vol. 1,* 8.

28. Ibid, 8-9

29. Jay P. Dolan, *New York's Irish and German Catholics, 1815-1865*, 2.

30. Charles Morris, *The Saints and Sinners Who Built America's Most Powerful Church*, 40.

31. Ibid, 41.

32. The Reverend Henry A. Bran, Most *Reverend John Hughes*, 86.

33. Quoted inRay Allen Billington, *The Protestant Crusade 1800-1860: A Study of the Origins of American Nativism*, (New York: Quadrangle Books, 1964), 143.

34. David O'Brien, *Public Catholicism*, (Chicago: McMillan Publishing Co.), 44.

35. Ibid, 45.

36. *Documents of the Assembly of the State of New York, 63rd Session, 1840*, Document No. 2, 5-6.

37. Lawrence Kehoe, ed.. *Complete Works of the Most Rev. John Hughes, D.D., Archbishop of New York*, Vol. 1, 102.

38. Ibid, 44.

39. Locofocos - The name of the workingmen's wing of the Democratic Party in New York City, who took their name from a meeting in Tammany Hall on October 29th, 1835. The party regulars had nominated their own slate of candidates for the upcoming municipal elections and declared the meeting adjourned. When disaffected workers

tried to contest the outcome and further prolong the meeting, the gas lights were turned out. The dissenters, however, had come prepared with the newest sulfur friction matches called "locofocos," or "lucifers."

40. Don Seitz, *The James Gordon Bennetts, Father and Son, Proprietors of New York* (New York: Houghton Mifflin, 1959), 107.

41. Alan Nevins and Milton Halsey Thomas, ed. *The Diary of George Templeton Strong: Young Man in New York, 1835-1849* (New York, The MacMillan Company, 1952), 177-178.

42. Ibid, p. 83.

43. *New York Daily Tribune*, November 6th, 1843.

44. David Potter, *The Impending Crisis 1848-1861: Completed and Edited by Don E. Fehrenbacher* (New York: Harper Row Publishers, Inc., 1976), 244-246.

45. Charles Morris, *The Saints and Sinners Who Built America's Most Powerful Church*, 44.

46. Nathan Glazer and Daniel P. Moynihan, *Beyond the Melting Pot*, 237.

47. Ibid, 237.

48. Ibid, 238.

49. Lawrence Kehoe, ed., *Complete Works of the Rev. John Hughes, D.D., Archbishop of New York, Vol. 1*, 318.

50. The Reverend Henry A. Bran, *Most Reverend John Hughes*, 96.

51. Ibid, 97-98., Quoted in Reverend Henry A. Bran.

52. Quoted in Daniel Walker Howe, *What Hath God Wrought: The Transformation of America, 1815-1845*, 769.

53. Allan Nevins, ed., *Polk: The Diary of a President, 1845-1849*, 97-98.

54. *Church Times*, June 9th, 1846; *New York Freeman's Journal*, June 13th, 1846.

55. *New York Herald Tribune*, July 2nd, 1846.

56. Sister Blanche Marie McEniry, M.A., "American Catholics in the War with Mexico" (PhD diss., Gettysburg Times and News Publishing Co., 1937), 41-42.

57. Lawrence Kehoe, ed. *Complete Works of the Rev. John J. Hughes, D.D., Archbishop of New York, Vol. 1*, 559.

58. Ibid, 559.

59. Ibid, 578.

60. Ibid, 578.

61. David Gibson, "St. *Brigid's Parish, A Pilgrim Church for an Immigrant People:*" Catholics in New York, Society, Culture and Politics, 1808-1946, ed. Terry Golway (New York: Fordham University Press, 2008), 55-57.

Chapter 4

I Know Nothing

1. Kenneth J. Zanca, ed., *American Catholics and Slavery: 1789-1866* (New York: University Press of America, 1994), 36.

2. Ibid, 36.

3. *The New York Times*, July 28th, 1855.

4. Ibid.

5. John T Ridge, edited by Lynn Mosher Bushnell, *Celebrating 250 Years of the Saint Patrick's Day Parade* (Hamden, Ct.: The Quinipiac University Press in Concert with the St. Patrick's Day Parade Committee, 2011), 14.

6. *The New York Times*, March 19th, 1855.

7. *The New York Times*, March 21st, 1855.

8. Ibid.

9. Pat McNamara, *What is a "Know-Nothing"? Anti-Catholicism was once so acceptable in America you could buy candy promoting it.*, August 15th, 2011.
    http://www.patheos.com/Resources/Additional-Resources/Know-Nothing-Pat-McNamara.

10. Ibid.

11. Charles Morris, *The Saints and Sinners Who Built America's Most Powerful Church*, 62.

12. *Louisville Courier*, July 20th, 1855.

13. Charles Morris, *The Saints and Sinners Who Built America's Most Powerful Church*, 62

14. Ibid, p. 63.

15. Allan Nevins and Milton Halsey Thomas, ed., *The Diary of George Templeton Strong: Young Man in New York, 1835-1849*

16. Lawrence Kehoe, ed., *Complete Works of the Most Reverend John Hughes, D.D., Archbishop of New York, Comprising His Sermons, Letters, Lectures, Speeches, Vol. 2*, 573.

17. Ibid, 593-594.

18. Alan Nevins and Milton Halsey Thomas, ed., *The Diary of George Templeton Strong: The Turbulent Years, 1850-1859* (New York: The MacMillan Company, 1952), 240.

19. Lawrence Kehoe, ed., *Complete Works of the Most Reverend John Hughes, D.D., Archbishop of New York, Vol. 2*, 595.

20. Quoted in Charles R. Morris, *The Saints and Sinners Who Built American's Most Powerful Church*, 75.

21. Leo Hershkowitz, "The Irish and the Emerging City, Settlement to 1844," 32.

22. Ibid, 32., Quoted in Leo Hershkowitz.

23. Ibid, 33.

24. Daniel Walker Howe, *What Hath God Wrought: The Transformation of America, 1815-1845*, 827.

25. Don Seitz, *The James Gordon Bennetts: Father and Son, Proprietors of New York*, 108-109.

26. James McPherson, *Battle Cry of Freedom* (New York: Oxford University Press, 1988), 157.

27. "Faugh A Ballagh" - Translated from the Irish language... "Clear the Way."

28. John Higham, *Stranger in the Land: Patterns of American Nativism 1860-1925*, 12.

Chapter 5

Stars And Stripes Washed In The Blood Of Kings

1. David Potter, *The Impending Crisis, 1848-1861*, 450-451.

2. Ibid, 439-440.

3. Doris Kearns Goodwin, *Team of Rivals: The Political Genius of Abraham Lincoln* (New York: Simon and Schuster, 2005), 247-250.

4. Lawrence Kehoe, ed. *Complete Works of the Rev. John J. Hughes, D.D., Archbishop of New York,*

Comprising His Sermons, Letters, Lectures, Speeches, etc., Vol. 2, 756.

5. Kenneth J. Zanca, ed., *American Catholics and Slavery: 1789-1866*, 246.

6. Ibid, p.247.

7. David Potter, *The Impending Crisis, 1848-1861*, 582-583.

8. *The New York Times*, April 20th, 1861.

9. Quoted in Edward K. Spann, "Union Green, the Irish Community and the Civil War:" *The New York Irish*, Ronald H. Bayor and Timothy J. Meagher, ed., 193-195.

10. Ibid, p.196.

11. Ibid, p.197.

12. Ibid, 199.

13. Abraham Lincoln Papers at the Library of Congress. Transcribed and Annotated by the Lincoln Studies Center, Knox College. Galesburg, Illinois. (Letter from Abraham Lincoln to John Hughes [Draft], October 21st, 1861).

14. Rena Mazyck Andrews, "Archbishop John Hughes and the Civil War." PhD diss, University of Chicago Press, 1935), 14.

15. Doris Kearns Goodwin, *Team of Rivals: The Political Genius of Abraham Lincoln*, 396-400.

16. Lawrence Kehoe, ed., *Complete Works of Rev. John J. Hughes, Vol. 2*, 761.

17. Ibid, p. 762.

18. Thurlow Weed Barnes, editor, Memoir of Thurlow Weed, Volume II, 350-351.

19. Rena Mazyck Andrews, "Archbishop John Hughes and the Civil War" 7-8.

20. James McPherson, *Battle Cry of Freedom*, 607.

21. Allan Nevins and Milton Halsey Thomas, ed., *The Diary of George Templeton Strong; The Civil War: 1860-1865* (New York MacMillan Company, 1952), 335.

22. James McPherson, *The Battle Cry of Freedom*, 610.

23. Quoted in Frank Klement, Author, Steven K. Rogstad, Editor, *Lincoln's Critics: The Copperheads of the North*, 105.

24. "Annals of the War Written by Leading Participants North and South," Originally published in the *Philadelphia Weekly Times*, p. 302 (T.P. McElrath, "The Draft Riots in New York").

25. William Allan Bates, *Tiger In The Streets: A City In A Time of Trouble*, 147.

26. John Tyler Headley, *The Great Riots of New York City*, 256-257.

27. Extract from "Parochial Record" - Diocese of Clogher, by Rev. J.E. McKenna, P.P., Printed at the "Fermanagh Herald" Office, Enniskillen, 1920.

28. Allan Nevins and Milton Halsey Thomas, *The Diary of George Templeton Strong: The Civil War, 1860-1865*, 390.

Chapter 6

"They May Do What They Like With The Diocese When I Am Under The Ground."

1. Jay P. Dolan, *New York's Irish and German Catholics, 1815-1865*, 70.

2. Ibid, 72.

3. Ibid, 72.

4. Quoted in Thomas J. Shelley, "Archbishop John Hughes and the Church in New York."

5. Quoted in Charles R. Morris, *American Catholic, The Saints and Sinners Who Built America's Most Powerful Church*, 75.

6. Cortes - Spanish parliament composed of a lower house (Congresso de los Diputados) and upper house (Senado). Although they share legislative power, the Congresso de los Diputados holds the power to override the Senado with a three-fifths or absolute majority.

7. *The Catholic Church in New York* (2 Volumes; New York and Boston, 1905), I, 78.

8. Ibid, I, 78.

9. Hasia R. Diner, "The Most Irish City in the Union:" The Era of the Great Migration, *The New York Irish*, ed. Ronald H. Baylor and Timothy J. Meagher, 105.

10. Quoted in Henry A. Bran, *The Most Reverend John Hughes*, 106.

11. Ibid, 106.

12. Charles Morris, *The Saints and Sinners Who Built America's Most Powerful Church*, 68.

13. *The New York Times*, November 1st, 1862.

14. Charles Morris, *The Saints and Sinners Who Built America's Most Powerful Church*, 84.

15. John Cooney: *American Pope: The Life and Times of Francis Cardinal Spellman* (New York: Times Publishing, 1984), Introduction.

16. Charles Morris, *The Saints and Sinners Who Built America's Most Powerful Church*, 84.

17. Ibid, 85.

18. Ibid, 85.

19. Tyler Anbinder, "Saving Grace, The Emigrant Savings Bank and its Depositors," *Catholics in*

New York: Society, Culture and Politics, 1808-1846, ed. Terry Golway, 83.

20. Ibid, 83.

21. Ibid.

22. Henry A. Bran, *The Most Reverend John Hughes*, 134.

23. Ibid, 134.

24. Ibid, 148.

Selected Bibliography

Andrews, Rena, Mazyck, "Archbishop John Hughes and the Civil War" (PhD diss., University of Chicago, 1935).

Abraham Lincoln Papers at the Library of Congress. Transcribed and Annotated by the Lincoln Studies Center, Knox College, Galesburg, Illinois.

Barnes, Thurlow Weed, editor, *Memoir of Thurlow Weed, Volume II.* Boston: Houghton-Miflin, 1st Edition, 1884.

Bayor, Ronald H. and Meagher, Timothy J., ed. *The New York Irish.* Baltimore: The John Hopkins University Press, 1996.

Bates, William Allan. *Tiger in the Streets: A City in Time of Trouble.* New York: 1966.

Billington, Ray Allen. *The Protestant Crusade 1800-1860: A Study of the Origins of American Nativism.* New York: Quadrangle Books, 1964.

Brann, Henry, A., *Most Rev. John Hughes: First Archbishop of New York.* New York: Dodd, Mead and Company, 1892.

Caesar, Gaius Julius. *Caesar's War Commentaries: De Bello Gallico and De Bello Civili*, New York: Kessinger Publishing, 2000.

Condon, Edward, O'Meagher. *The Irish Race in America.* New York: Ogham Press, Inc., 1976.

Cooney, John. *American Pope: The Life and Times of Francis Cardinal Spellman.* New York: Times Books, 1984.

Crossman, Virginia. *Politics, Law and Order in 19th Century Ireland.* Dublin: Gill & MacMillan Ltd., 1996.

Documents of the Assembly of the State of New York, 63rd Session, 1840, Document No. #2.

Dolan, Jay P. *The Immigrant Church: New York's Irish and German Catholics, 1815-1865.* Baltimore: John Hopkins University Press, 1977.

Glazer, Nathan and Moynihan, Daniel P., *Beyond The Melting Pot: The Negroes, Puerto Ricans, Jews, Italians and Irish of New York City.* Cambridge: MIT Press, 1970.

Golway, Terry, ed. *Catholics in New York: Society, Culture and Politics, 1808-1946.* New York: Fordham University Press, 2008.

Goodwin, Doris Kearns. *Team of Rivals: The Political Genius of Abraham Lincoln.* New York, Simon and Schuster, 2005.

Handlin, Oscar. *The Uprooted.* New York: Grosset and Dunlap Publishers, 1951.

Hansen, Marcus L., *The Atlantic Migration: 1607-1860*. Cambridge, Cambridge University Press, 1940.

Headley, Tyler, John. *The Great Riots of New York City: 1712 to 1873*. Kila, Montana: Kessigner Publishing Company, 2010.

Higham, John, *Strangers in The Land: Patterns of American Nativism*, 1860-1925, New York: Atheneum, 1963.

Howe, Daniel, Walker. *What Hath God Wrought: The Transformation of America, 1815-1848*, New York: Oxford University Press, 2007.

Kehoe, Lawrence., ed. *Complete Works of the Most Rev. John Hughes, D.D., Archbishop of New York, Comprising His Sermons, Letters, Lectures, Speeches, Etc., Vol. 1*. New York: Lawrence Kehoe, 7 Beekman Street; 1866.

Kehoe, Lawrence., ed. *Complete Works of the Most Rev. John Hughes, D.D., Archbishop of New York, Comprising His Sermons, Letters, Lectures, Speeches, Etc., Vol. 2*. New York: Lawrence Kehoe, 7 Beekman Street; 1866.

Killin, John, *The Famine Decade: Contemporary Accounts 1841-1851*, Belfast: Blackstaff Press, 1995.

Klement, Frank. Author. Rogstad, Steven K. Editor. *Lincoln's Critics: The Copperheads of the North*. Shippensberg: White Mane Publishing Co., Inc., 1999.

Lenon, Colm. *Sixteenth-Century Ireland: The Incomplete Conquest.* Dublin: Gill and McMillan, Ltd., 1994.

Litton, Helen. *The Irish Famine: An Illustrated History.* Dublin: Wolfhound Press, 1994.

Lyons, F.S.L. *Ireland Since the Famine.* London: Fontana Press, 1963.

Martin, F.X. and Moody, T.W., ed. *The Course of Irish History.* Cork: Mercier Press, 1967.

McEniry, Sister Blanche Marie, M.A., "American Catholics in the War With Mexico." (PhD diss., Washington, D.C. The Catholic University of America, 1937).

McPherson, James. *Battle Cry of Freedom.* New York: Oxford University Press, 1988.

Monahan, Jay. *Diplomat in Carpet Slippers.* Chicago: Chicago University Press, 1968.

Morris, Charles, R. *American Catholic: The Saints and Sinners Who Built America's Most Powerful Church.* New York: Times Books, 1977.

Nevins, Allan and Thomas, Milton Halsey, ed. *The Diary of George Templeton Strong: Young Man in New York, 1835-1849.* New York: The McMillan Company, 1952.

Nevins, Allan and Thomas, Milton Halsey, ed. *The Diary of George Templeton Strong: The Turbulent Fifties, 1850-1859.* New York: The McMillan Company, 1952.

Nevins, Allan and Thomas, Milton Halsey, ed. *The Diary of George Templeton Strong: The Civil War, 1860-1865.* New York: The McMillan Company, 1952.

Nevins, Allan, ed. *Polk: The Diary of a President, 1845-1849.* New York: Capricorn Books, 1929.

O'Brien, David. *Public Catholicism.* Chicago: McMillan Publishing Co., 1962.

O'Brien, Maire and Conor Cruise. *A Concise History of Ireland.* New York: Bekman House, 1972.

Póirtéir, Cathal, ed. *The Great Irish Famine,* Dublin: Mercier Press, 1995.

Potter, David. M., *The Impending Crisis 1848-1861: Completed and Edited by Don E. Fehrenbacher.* New York: Harper & Row Publishers, Inc., 1976.

Rayback, Robert J., *Millard Fillmore,* Buffalo: Buffalo Historical Society, 1959.

Ridge, John T., *Celebrating 250 Years of the Saint Patrick's Day Parade,* ed. Lynn Mosher Bushnell. New York: The Quinnipiac Press, 2011.

Robinson, Philip, *The Plantation of Ulster.* St. Martin's Press, 1984.

Sandburg, Carl. *Abraham Lincoln: The Prairie Years and The War Years, One Volume Edition.* New York: Harcourt, Brace & Company, 1954.

Seitz, Don. *The James Gordon Bennetts: Father and Son, Proprietors of New York.* New York: Houghton, Mifflin, 1959.

Shaw, Richard. *Dagger John, The Unquiet Life and Times of Archbishop John Hughes of New York.* New York: Paulist Press, 1977.

Zanca, Kenneth L., *American Catholics and Slavery: 1789-1866.* New York: University Press of America, 1994.

Articles

McNamara, Patrick, Dr., "What Is A Know-Nothing"?, August 15th, 2011, http://www.patheos.com/Resources/Additional-Resources/Know-Nothing-Pat-McNamara.

McNamara, Robert, "Archbishop John Hughes Led the Irish in the 19th Century: An Immigrant Priest Wielded Power in America," http://history1800's.about.com/od/americanoriginals/a/a/revjohnhughes.htm.

Shelley, Thomas, J., "Archbishop John Hughes and the Church in New York" Catholic New York, July 6th, 2000, http://cnv.org/archive/ft/ft070600.htm.

Stern, William J., "How Dagger John Saved New York's Irish," City Journal, Spring, 1997, http://www.city-journal.org/html7/2a2.html.

Index

A

B

C

T

Tacitus, Publius, Cornelius, 47
Trusteeism, 40

V

Varella, *Father Felix y Morales*, 129, 130

W

Weed, Thurlow, xvii, 7, 66, 81, 92, 114
Wellington, *Duke of*, 30, 31
Whigs, 56, 64, 65, 66
Whore of Babylon, 42
Wilkes, John, *Captain*, 115

X

Xenophobic fears, xii